SIDE by SIDE

ACTIVITY WORKBOOK

Second Edition

3

Steven J. Molinsky
Bill Bliss

Contributing Authors

Elizabeth Handley / Katharine Kolowich / with Mary Ann Perry

PRENTICE HALL REGENTS   Englewood Cliffs, New Jersey 07632

Editorial/production supervision: Janet Johnston
Art supervision: Karen Salzbach
Manufacturing buyer: Peter Havens
Cover design: Kenny Beck

Illustrated by Richard E. Hill

 © 1989 by Prentice-Hall Inc.
A Division of Simon & Schuster
Englewood Cliffs, New Jersey 07632

Printed in the United States of America

10 9 8 7 6 5 4 3 2

ISBN 0-13-811795-0

Prentice-Hall International (UK) Limited, *London*
Prentice-Hall of Australia Pty. Limited, *Sydney*
Prentice-Hall Canada Inc., *Toronto*
Prentice-Hall Hispanoamericana, S.A., *Mexico*
Prentice-Hall of India Private Limited, *New Delhi*
Prentice-Hall of Japan, Inc. *Tokyo*
Simon & Schuster Asia Pte. Ltd., *Singapore*
Editora Prentice-Hall do Brasil, Ltda., *Rio de Janeiro*

CONTENTS

A. WHAT'S HAPPENING?

What	bake	drink	go	plant
Where	buy	eat	move	swim

1. ___What's___ Mrs. Green ___drinking___ ?

   ___She's drinking___ coffee.

2. _____ Jennifer _____ ?

   _____ to a concert.

3. _____ Mr. Williams _____ ?

   _____ flowers.

4. _____ you and your friend

   _____ ?

   _____ ice cream.

5. _____ Mr. and Mrs. Hardy _____ ?

   _____ to Centerville.

6. _____ you _____ ?

   _____ a chocolate

   cake.

7. _____ Mr. and Mrs. Jones _____ ?

   _____ presents for

   their children.

8. _____ Roger _____ ?

   _____ at the beach.

1

B. ON THE PHONE

1. Hi. What ___are___ you doing?

   _____ dinner.

   I'm sorry. I always call at the wrong time. _____ Tom busy?

   Yes, _____. _____ a shower. Can we call you later?

   Sure. I'll be home all evening.

2. Hi. _____ you and Harry doing today?

   Not very much. Right now _____ reading.

   Why don't we all go to a concert together?

   That's a great idea.

3. Hello, Janet. _____ the children okay?

   Yes. _____ fine.

   What _____ they doing?

   Mary _____ for her English examination, and

   the boys _____ TV.

   Tell them I'll be home soon.

4.

Hello, Jim. This is Uncle Ted. _____ your father there?

No, he isn't. _____ late at the office.

May I speak to your mother?

I'm afraid she can't come to the phone right now. _____ very busy.

Really? _____ doing?

_____ the sink. It's broken.

That's too bad. I guess I'll call back later.

5.

Hello, ... Can I speak to ....?

I'm sorry. ....
....

Well, can I speak to ....?

I'm afraid ....
....

I guess I'll call back later.

C. YOU DECIDE: *Why Is Today Different?*

1. (clean)   I never _____*clean*_____ my apartment, but _____*I'm cleaning*_____ my apartment

   today because *my parents are going to visit* (or) *my boss is coming over for dinner*.

2. (wear)   George never _____ a tie, but _____ a tie today

   because ....

3. (work)   We never _____ late at the office, but _____ late today

   because ....

4. (argue)   Michael never _____ with his brother, but _____ with

   him right now because ....

5. (send)   Mario never _____ his girlfriend flowers, but _____

   her flowers today because ....

6. (study)   Elizabeth never _____ , but _____ today

   because ....

7. (take)   Mr. and Mrs. Smith never _____ the subway, but _____

   the subway today because ....

8. (watch)   Our teacher never _____ TV, but _____ TV today

   because ....

9. (write)   My older brother never _____ to our family, but _____

   to us today because ....

10. (get up)   Janet never _____ early, but _____ early today

    because ....

11. (drink)   Mr. and Mrs. Jones never _____ champagne, but _____

    champagne today because ....

12. (go)   Susan never _____ to restaurants, but _____ to a

    restaurant today because ....

13. (smile)   Mr. Sharp never _____ , but _____ today

    because ....

D. WHAT ARE THEY SAYING?

1. Lois plays the piano beautifully.

   ___Does___ her daughter also ___play___ the piano well?

2. My brother lives in Chicago.

   _____ your sister _____ there, too?

3. My son gets up at 6:00 every morning.

   _____ you _____ early, too?

4. Our daughter goes to the movies every week.

   _____ you and your wife _____ to the movies very often?

5. Robert likes classical music.

   _____ he _____ popular music, too?

6. Tommy and Nancy watch TV all afternoon.

   _____ they _____ TV in the evening?

7. Hilda bakes delicious bread.

   _____ cookies, too?

8. Alice and I usually walk to work.

   _____ to work in the winter?

9. Boris speaks French and Russian.

   _____ English, too?

10. William and Richard work at night.

    _____ during the day?

11. Norman has two grandsons.

    _____ any granddaughters?

12. Frieda and Julie always complain about school.

    _____ about their teacher?

13. I drink three cups of coffee every morning.

    _____ a lot of coffee in the afternoon, too?

14. Margaret always worries about her daughter.

    _____ about her son?

E. WHAT'S THE WORD?

1. I ___don't___ like to go dancing with Peter because he _____ a good dancer.

   I know. Everybody says _____ very clumsy.

2. My sister _____ a very good singer.

   I don't agree with you. I think she _____ beautifully. _____ very talented.

3. My mother _____ like to ride to work with me because she thinks _____ a terrible driver. She's wrong! I _____ very carefully.

4. Shirley _____ going swimming with us today because she _____ like to swim when it's cold.

   That's too bad. I really like to go swimming with her. She's an excellent _____.

5. My husband and I _____ very good skaters, but we like to _____ anyway.

   _____ you like to ski?

   No, we _____. _____ afraid we might get hurt.

6. I'm really jealous of my brothers.

   Why?

   Because _____ very good athletes, and I'm not.

   Don't be ridiculous! Your brothers _____ tennis very well, but you're a good tennis _____, too.

   _____ you really think so?

   Of course I _____.

6

F. LISTEN

Listen to each question and then complete the answer.

1. Yes, _____*he does*_____ ,
2. Yes, _____*she is*_____ .
3. Yes, _____ .
4. Yes, _____ .
5. No, _____ .

6. No, _____ .
7. Yes, _____ .
8. No, _____ .
9. Yes, _____ .
10. Yes, _____ .

11. No, _____ .
12. Yes, _____ .
13. No, _____ .
14. No, _____ .
15. Yes, _____ .

G. WHAT'S THE QUESTION?

1. He's writing to <u>his sister</u>. _____*Who's he writing to?*_____

2. They're visiting <u>their friends</u>. _____

3. She's complaining about <u>her examination</u>. _____

4. I'm calling <u>my boss</u>. _____

5. She's thinking about <u>her new job</u>. _____

6. He's shouting at <u>his landlord</u>. _____

7. We're waiting for <u>the bus</u>. _____

8. They're talking about <u>their vacation</u>. _____

9. He's arguing with <u>his son</u>. _____

10. I'm writing about <u>my favorite movie</u>. _____ ?

7

H. WHAT ARE THEY SAYING?

1. A. Why is Tom visiting ___his___ aunt?

    B. ___He___ wants to tell ___her___ about this afternoon's football game.

2. A. Why is Mrs. Brown calling _____ neighbors?

    B. _____ wants to tell _____ about _____ vacation.

3. A. Why are David and Frank complaining about _____ teacher, Mrs. Stotter?

    B. _____ gives _____ too much homework.

4. A. Why are you calling _____ friend Peter so late?

    B. _____ want to talk to _____ about tomorrow's examination.

5. A. Why are you and _____ friends studying so late?

    B. If _____ don't finish this book tonight, _____ teacher will be angry at _____ .

6. A. Why is Mrs. Watson writing to _____ son?

    B. _____ wants to wish _____ "Happy Birthday."

7. A. What are your parents giving _____ for your birthday, Johnny?

    B. I'm not sure, but _____ might give _____ an electric train.

8. A. Why is Mr. Young shouting at _____ daughter?

    B. _____ forgot to ask _____ before she took the car this afternoon.

9.

    I want to tell _____ and Dad about the party last night.

    Go back to sleep! You can tell _____ about _____ later.

8

I. WHAT'S THE WORD?

1. Carmen always complains [at / (about)] the weather in Chicago.

2. Call [to / at] the plumber right away!

3. Why is Jim arguing [at / to / with] his little sister?

4. Judy writes [at / to / from] her boyfriend twice a week.

5. Mrs. Morgan doesn't like to shout [at / to / ---] her children.

6. Mrs. Lopez visits [at / to / ---] her sister whenever she goes [at / to / ---] Miami.

7. I'm helping [at / to / ---] my daughter [to / with / ---] her homework.

8. Mr. Crabapple is frustrated because he has to wait [for / --- / at] the bus.

9. Why does Charlie always talk [at / --- / about] his problems?

10. My parents are watching [to / --- / at] their favorite TV program.

11. Who's feeding [to / at / ---] the dog today?

9

A. A TERRIBLE NIGHTMARE

It (be) ___was___ midnight, and I (be) _____ at a party at a friend's house
when the babysitter (call) _____. "Come home right away!" she said.

    I didn't stop to ask any questions. I (get) _____ into my car and (drive)
_____ home as quickly as possible. But when I (reach) _____
River Street, the most dangerous street in town, I (get) _____ a flat tire.

    It (be) _____ very dark and quiet, and I (be) _____ terribly afraid.
I (start) _____ to walk down the street, when I (see) _____ an
enormous dog. He (look) _____ very angry, and he (bark)
_____ when he (see) _____ me. What (can) _____ I do?
I (have) _____ to think quickly. Fortunately, I (have) _____ some food from
the party with me. I (take) _____ some cookies from my pocket, and I (give)
_____ them to the dog. He (stop) _____ barking right away, and he
(eat) _____ the cookies. While he was eating, I (walk) _____ away.

    A half hour later, I finally (arrive) _____ home. I (look)
_____ in my pocket for the key, but it wasn't there. I guess I (lose)
_____ it when I was feeding the dog. I (decide) _____ to get into the
house through the living room window.

    A few minutes later, I (be) _____ in the living room. I didn't see or hear
anything strange, so I (go) _____ upstairs. Then somebody (shout)

_____ , "Help!" I (be) _____ so nervous that I (trip) _____
    29   30   31
over a chair and (fall) _____ down. Then ....
                          32
....
....
....
....
....

I'm glad it was only a dream.

B. LISTEN

Listen and put a circle around the correct words.

1.	yesterday / (every day)	6.	last Friday / every Friday	11.	yesterday / every day
2.	(yesterday evening) / every evening	7.	yesterday morning / every morning	12.	yesterday / every day
3.	yesterday / every day	8.	last night / every night	13.	yesterday afternoon / every afternoon
4.	yesterday evening / every evening	9.	last week / every week	14.	yesterday evening / every evening
5.	last week / every week	10.	yesterday morning / every morning	15.	yesterday morning / every morning

C. LISTEN

Listen and fill in the missing words.   Then read the passage aloud.

My parents ___*needed*___ a lot of help when they moved to their new house.   I _____
                    1   2

heavy furniture for them, and I _____ all the rooms.   When I _____ one day, my
                                 3   4

mother said she _____ a garden.   I _____ until spring, and then I _____
                5   6   7

one.   I _____ flowers and vegetables in the yard.
        8

Yesterday my brother _____ to move.   I'm not complaining.   I really like to help.
                     9

But I think I'll be busy for a while!

D. WHAT'S THE QUESTION?

1. _____*Did you go*_____ to the movies?   No, I didn't.   I went to a concert.

2. _____ anything for me?   No, I didn't.   I bought something for your
                                                     mother.

3. _____ her glasses?   No, she didn't.   She forgot her purse.

4. _____ German?   No, he didn't.   He taught French.

5. _____ by plane?   No, they didn't.   They came by train.

6. _____ a stomachache?   No, she didn't.   She had a cold.

7. _____ Martin?   No, I didn't.   I saw his sister.

8. _____ his English   No, he didn't.   He did his math homework.
   homework?

9. _____ your cassette   No, they didn't.   They stole our money.
   player?

10. _____ a red   No, I didn't.   I lost a blue one.
    umbrella?

E. SOMETHING DIFFERENT

1. David usually has yogurt for lunch.

   He _____didn't_____ _____have_____ yogurt for lunch yesterday.

   He ____had____ a salad.

2. Barbara usually sits by herself in English class.

   She _____ _____ by herself yesterday.

   She _____ with her friends.

3. We usually buy ice cream for dessert.

   We _____ _____ ice cream yesterday.

   We _____ strawberries.

4. Our music teacher usually sings very well.

   She _____ _____ very well yesterday.

   She _____ badly.

5. Sally and Carl usually go to work by car.

   They _____ _____ to work by car yesterday.

   They _____ to work by taxi.

6. I usually drink a lot of coffee.

   I _____ _____ any coffee yesterday.

   I _____ a lot of tea.

7. My grandmother usually gives me a tie for my birthday.

   She _____ _____ me a tie this year.

   She _____ me a shirt.

8. Eleanor usually takes a ballet lesson on Tuesday.

   She _____ _____ a ballet lesson last Tuesday.

   She _____ a piano lesson.

9. We usually get home at 5:00.

   We _____ _____ home at 5:00 yesterday.

   We _____ home very late.

10. Irene usually drives carefully.

    She _____ _____ carefully yesterday.

    She _____ much too fast.

11. Ted usually rides his motorcycle.

    He _____ _____ his motorcycle yesterday.

    He _____ his bicycle.

12. Mr. Warren usually teaches science.

    He _____ _____ science this year.

    He _____ math.

F. WHAT ARE THEY SAYING?

1. _____*Did you clean*_____ the basement?

No, _____. I _____ too tired. But I cleaned my room.

2. _____ to Albert yesterday?

No, I _____. I talked to his wife.

Albert _____ there when I called.

3. _____ you see Paul at the party last Saturday?

No, we _____. But we _____ his wife.

4. _____ you write to Mr. Jones yesterday?

No, I _____. I _____ too busy.

But I _____ to Mr. Henderson.

5. _____ Peggy _____ her motorcycle to work this morning?

No, she _____. She rode her bicycle, and she _____ late.

14

6. _____ you read Chapter One last night?

Yes, _____. _____ it twice because it _____ so interesting.

7. _____ Mrs. Nelson teach English last year?

Yes, _____. And she _____ history, too.

_____ you in her class?

No, we _____.

8. _____ the children eat a big lunch?

Yes, _____. They _____ so hungry that they _____ three sandwiches.

9. _____ buy anything at the store?

Yes, I _____. _____ some food for tonight.

_____ any oranges?

No, I didn't. There _____ any fresh ones.

10. What's the matter? _____ hurt you back?

No, I _____. _____ my arm.

I guess I _____ very careful.

15

G. HOW DID IT HAPPEN?

1. How did Alice hurt herself?   (play soccer)

   _____ *She hurt herself while she was playing soccer.* _____

2. How did Martin burn himself?   (iron his clothes)

   _____

3. How did Helen cut herself?   (slice onions)

   _____

4. How did Jennifer meet her husband?   (fix a flat tire)

   _____

5. How did Marvin break his arm?   (skate)

   _____

6. How did you lose your wallet?   (ride my bicycle)

   _____

7. How did Jeff meet his wife?   (swim at the beach)

   _____

8. How did Bob get a black eye?   (fight with his brother)

   _____

9. How did your children burn themselves?   (make breakfast)

   _____

10. How did Martha trip and fall?   (dance)

    _____

11. How did you ....?

    ....

    That's too bad.

H. WHAT'S THE QUESTION?

how	what	where
how long	what kind of	who
how many	when	why

1. _____ *Who did you visit* _____ ? I visited <u>my cousin</u>.

2. _____ ? We talked about <u>my job</u>.

3. _____ ? She went <u>to the beach</u>.

4. _____ ? She met <u>her friend</u>.

5. _____ ? They spoke <u>Russian</u>.

6. _____ ? They swam <u>in the ocean</u>.

7. _____ ? He had dinner <u>at 8:00</u>.

8. _____ ? I baked an <u>apple</u> pie.

9. _____ ? She cried <u>because her dog ran away</u>.

10. _____ ? I stayed <u>for a week</u>.

11. _____ ? I came home <u>by train</u>.

12. _____ ? He ate <u>three</u> hamburgers.

13. _____ ? He left the restaurant <u>at 9:00</u>.

14. _____ They covered their eyes <u>because they</u>

    _____ ? <u>were scared</u>.

15. _____ ? She wrote a letter to <u>her mother</u>.

16. _____ ? They studied <u>all morning</u>.

17. _____ ? We took a <u>lot of</u> photographs.

18. _____ ? We sent a postcard to <u>our teacher</u>.

19. _____ ? He fell asleep <u>during the lecture</u>.

20. _____ ? I lost my wallet <u>while I was skating</u>.

I. A VACATION

Use these pictures as a guide to write about a vacation.

J. SOUND IT OUT

Listen to each word and then say it.

<u>this:</u>

1. v<u>i</u>sit
2. W<u>i</u>lliam
3. mus<u>i</u>c
4. f<u>i</u>sh
5. b<u>u</u>sy
6. <u>i</u>sn't

<u>these:</u>

1. w<u>ee</u>kend
2. b<u>ea</u>ch
3. happ<u>y</u>
4. rec<u>ei</u>ve
5. St<u>e</u>ve
6. <u>ea</u>sy

Listen and put a circle around the word that has the same sound.

1. f<u>i</u>nish:	f<u>i</u>ne	(w<u>i</u>nter)	p<u>i</u>zza
2. s<u>i</u>t:	<u>i</u>nteresting	<u>i</u>ron	<u>ea</u>t
3. m<u>ea</u>t:	br<u>ea</u>d	br<u>ea</u>k	mov<u>ie</u>s
4. t<u>ee</u>th:	h<u>i</u>story	s<u>ee</u>	gr<u>ea</u>t
5. l<u>i</u>sten:	p<u>ie</u>ce	n<u>i</u>ght	d<u>i</u>d
6. st<u>ea</u>l:	dent<u>i</u>st	an<u>y</u>	w<u>ea</u>ther
7. l<u>i</u>ft:	L<u>i</u>nda	l<u>i</u>fe	f<u>ee</u>t
8. r<u>i</u>p:	sm<u>i</u>le	th<u>ie</u>f	th<u>i</u>s

Now make a sentence using all the words you circled.   Read the sentence aloud.

9. _____ _____ _____ _____ _____ _____

_____ _____

10. d<u>i</u>sh:	tr<u>i</u>cks	t<u>ea</u>ch	br<u>ie</u>fcase
11. gr<u>ee</u>n:	h<u>ea</u>lthy	w<u>ea</u>r	thr<u>ee</u>
12. m<u>i</u>x:	ch<u>i</u>ld	mag<u>i</u>c	pl<u>ea</u>se
13. n<u>ee</u>d:	Ir<u>e</u>ne	m<u>e</u>n	r<u>ea</u>dy
14. l<u>i</u>ttle:	exerc<u>i</u>se	<u>i</u>s	spaghett<u>i</u>
15. b<u>i</u>g:	pract<u>i</u>cing	w<u>i</u>ne	adv<u>i</u>ce
16. sw<u>i</u>m:	pol<u>i</u>ce	r<u>i</u>pe	d<u>i</u>fficult

Now make a sentence using all the words you circled.   Read the sentence aloud.

17. _____ _____ _____ _____ _____ _____

_____

A. WHAT ARE THEY SAYING?

3

1. Did we give our granddaughter a watch for her birthday this year?

   No, we didn't. We _gave_ her a gold bracelet. _We're going_ _to give_ her a watch next year.

2. Did your sister go out on a date with Robert last night?

   _____. She _____ out with Tom. _____ out with Robert tomorrow night.

3. Did you write an interesting story for homework today?

   _____. I _____ a very boring one. _____ a more interesting story next time.

4. Did Tom and Sheila drive to Los Angeles last weekend?

   _____. They _____ to San Francisco. _____ to Los Angeles next weekend.

5. Did you wear your new shoes to school yesterday?

   _____. I _____ my boots. _____ my new shoes tomorrow.

6. Did you and your friends read Shakespeare in class last semester?

   _____. We _____ Hemingway. _____ Shakespeare next semester.

7. Did Billy send a birthday present to Uncle Jim last week?

_____ . He _____ one to Uncle Barney. _____

_____ a birthday present to Uncle Jim next week.

8. Did you leave work early last night?

_____

I _____ work very late. _____

_____ work early tonight.

9. Did you do your English homework last night?

_____ . I _____ my Spanish homework.

_____ my English homework tonight.

10. Did you and Ronald eat at home last night?

_____ . We _____ at Stanley's International Restaurant. _____

_____ at home tonight.

11. Did you see the new science fiction movie at the Rix Theater last night?

_____ . I _____ a western at the Regency. _____

_____ the new science fiction movie at the Rix Theater tonight.

12. Did Mom and Dad speak to the landlord about our broken window?

_____ . They _____ to him about the cockroaches in the kitchen. _____

_____ to him about our broken window the next time they see him.

B. BAD CONNECTIONS

1. I'm so nervous. Tomorrow my doctor is going to #########

   I'm sorry. I can't hear you. I think we have a bad connection. What's _your doctor going to do_ ?

2. I'm really excited about my vacation. We're going to go ######

   What did you say? I can't hear you. Where _____ ?

3. My son is really disappointed. His best friend is going to move because ######

   I'm sorry. We have a terrible connection. Why _____ ?

4. My parents are going to give me a ######### for my twenty-first birthday.

   Excuse me. I can't hear you. _____ ?

5. My daughter is really looking forward to this Saturday night. She's going to go out with ##########

   We have a bad connection. _____ ?

6. Please come to our wedding. We're going to get married next #############

   I'm sorry. I can't hear you. _____ ?

7. I won't be home tomorrow. I'm going to visit ###### in the hospital.

   We have a very bad connection. _____ ?

8. Peggy and John are going to name their new baby ##########

    What did you say? I can't hear you very well. _____ _____?

9. Mr. Smith. I'm going to fire you because #### ##########

    Excuse me, sir. I think we have a bad connection. _____ _____ _____?

10. And after we steal the money, you and I are going to go ########

    What??!! I can't hear you. _____ _____?

C. I'M AFRAID

Michael is a pessimist. He always thinks the worst will happen.

1. I'm afraid I _____*won't have*_____ a good time at Robert's party this weekend.

2. I'm afraid my daughter ___*will*___

    ___*catch*___ a cold in the park today.

All his friends are optimists. They always tell Michael he shouldn't worry.

1. Yes, _____*you will*_____.

    We're sure ___*you'll*___ have a wonderful time!

2. No, _____*she won't*_____.

    ___*She won't*___ catch a cold today. She's wearing a warm sweater.

(continued)   23

3. I'm afraid my car _____ _____ on cold mornings this winter.

3. Yes, _____. We're sure _____ start every morning.

4. I'm afraid my children _____ _____ my birthday this year.

4. No, _____. We're sure _____ forget your birthday!

5. I'm afraid my landlord _____ _____ my broken sink.

5. Yes, _____. We're sure _____ fix it as soon as he can.

6. I'm afraid I _____ happy in my new job.

6. Of course _____. _____ be very happy in your new job.

7. I'm afraid my son _____ a car accident. It's raining very hard.

7. No, _____. We're sure _____ have an accident. He's a careful driver.

8. I'm afraid I _____ weight on my new diet.

8. Yes, _____. Of course _____ lose weight. Don't worry about it!

9. I'm afraid my wife _____ _____ my new haircut.

9. We're sure _____. _____ like your haircut a lot. You look terrific!

10. I'm afraid my neighbors _____ _____ angry because I'm having a big party tonight.

10. No, _____. _____ be angry. Why don't you invite them, too?

D. EVERYBODY'S BUSY

1. Will Jane be busy tonight?

   Yes, _____*she will*_____ .

   _____*She'll be studying*_____ English until ten o'clock.

2. Will you be busy this evening?

   Yes, _____ .

   _____ until 10 or 11 o'clock.

3. Will Mr. and Mrs. Morgan be busy today?

   Yes, _____ . _____

   _____

   until about 4:30.

4. Will Peggy be busy tomorrow morning?

   Yes, _____ . _____

   _____ all morning.

5. Will Frank be busy today?

   Yes, _____ . _____

   _____ all day.

6. Will Alan be busy after dinner?

   Yes, _____ . _____

   _____ for an hour or two.

7. Will your sister be busy this morning?

   Yes, _____ . _____

   _____ for several hours.

8. Will you and your husband be busy tonight?

   Yes, _____ . _____

   _____ at Franklin's International Night Club until midnight.

E. A TOUR OF MY CITY

Pretend you're taking people on a tour of your city or town. **Fill in the blanks with real places you know.**

Good morning, everybody.   This is .... speaking.   I'm so glad

you'll be coming with me today on a tour of ....   We'll be leaving in just

a few minutes.

First, I'll be taking you to see my favorite places in the city: ....,

...., and ....

Then we'll be going to .... for lunch.   In my opinion, this

is the best restaurant in town.   After that, I'll be taking you to see the other interesting tourist

sights: ...., ...,

and ....   This evening we'll be going to ....

....   I'm sure you'll have a wonderful time.

26

F. DID YOU HEAR?

mine
his
hers
ours
yours
theirs

ANNE: Did you hear what happened last night?

BETTY: No, I didn't. What happened?

ANNE: The police found a blue car in the park down the street. All the windows were broken

and the radio was missing. I hope that blue car isn't ___yours___.
1

BETTY: I don't think so. I'm sure my husband drove _____ to work this morning.
2

Could it be Mr. Anderson's car? _____ is blue.
3

ANNE: No. I don't think so. _____ is at the repair shop.
4

BETTY: How about Mrs. Taylor? Maybe it's _____. I think she has a blue car.
5

ANNE: No. I don't think so. _____ isn't blue. I think it's green.
6

BETTY: How about Mr. and Mrs. Lane? Don't they have an old blue car? Maybe it's _____.
7

ANNE: No. It can't be _____. They moved away last month.
8

BETTY: How about YOU, Anne? Are you SURE it isn't _____?
9

ANNE: I'm positive! I know it isn't _____. My car is in front of the house. Wait a
10

minute. I'll look out the window right now.

BETTY: Is it still there? Do you see it?

ANNE: Oh no! It isn't there. I'm afraid the car in the park might be _____.
11

BETTY: Maybe you should call the police.

G. WHAT DOES IT MEAN?

Put a circle around the correct answer.

1. He's composing a symphony.
   - a. He's writing a symphony.
   - b. He's listening to a symphony.
   - c. He's going to a concert.

2. Michael has a black eye.
   - a. He painted his eye.
   - b. He hurt his eye.
   - c. He's wearing dark glasses.

3. Barry wasn't on time.
   - a. He was early.
   - b. He was late.
   - c. He didn't have a good time.

4. I'm going to fill out my income tax form.
   - a. I'm going to return my income tax form.
   - b. I'm going to answer the questions on my income tax form.
   - c. I'm going to read my income tax form.

5. Can I borrow your hammer?
   - a. I need your hammer for a little while.
   - b. I want to give you my hammer.
   - c. I want to buy your hammer.

6. She wasn't prepared for her exam.
   - a. She didn't take her exam.
   - b. She didn't study for her exam.
   - c. She was ready for her exam.

7. I'm going to lend my car to Bill today.
   - a. I'm going to give my car to Bill.
   - b. I'm going to drive Bill's car.
   - c. Bill is going to give me his car.

8. Mr. Warren is looking forward to his retirement.
   - a. He's happy about his new job.
   - b. He wants to buy new tires for his car.
   - c. Soon he won't have to go to work every day.

9. My sister is arguing with her boyfriend.
    a. They're having a good time.
    b. They don't agree about something.
    c. They agree about something.

10. I'm going to repair my brother's bicycle.
    a. I'm going to paint it again.
    b. I'm going to fix it.
    c. I'm going to ride it.

11. Could you possibly do me a favor?
    a. I want to help you.
    b. I want to give you something.
    c. I need your help.

12. Edward is complaining to his boss.
    a. He's talking about his boss and he's very upset.
    b. He's talking to his boss and he's very happy.
    c. He's talking to his boss and he's very upset.

13. I'm going to call my husband right away.
    a. I'm going to call him immediately.
    b. I'm going to call him in a few hours.
    c. I'm going to call him when I have the time.

14. Sarah is looking for a magazine.
    a. She's looking for a store.
    b. She's looking for something to read.
    c. She's looking for the second floor.

15. My parents are going to relax this weekend.
    a. They're going to retire this weekend.
    b. They're going to exercise this weekend.
    c. They're going to rest this weekend.

□□ H. LISTEN: *Looking Forward*

Listen and answer the questions after each story.

What's Henry Looking Forward to?

1. _____
2. _____
3. _____

What's Bobby Looking Forward to?

1. _____
2. _____
3. _____
4. _____

What's Julie Looking Forward to?

1. _____
2. _____
3. _____
4. _____
5. _____

CHECK-UP TEST: *Chapters 1–3*

A. Fill in the blanks.

Ex. Mary ___*is*___ a good skier, and her

children ___*ski*___ well, too.

1. A. George and Peter _____ wonderful swimmers.

   B. I agree with you. They _____ very well.

2. A. Helen _____ carelessly.

   B. I know. _____ a terrible driver.

3. A. I don't skate very well.

   B. I don't agree with you. I think _____ an excellent _____ .

4. We _____ good tennis _____ , but we like to _____ tennis anyway.

B. Fill in the blanks.

1. A. Did you write to Mr. Jones yesterday?

   B. No, I _____ . I _____ too

   busy. But I _____ to Mr. Lee.

2. A. Did you buy any milk when you

   _____ at the store?

   B. No, I _____ . I forgot. But I

   _____ some orange juice.

3. A. _____ Mrs. Armstrong teach French last year?

   B. No, she _____ . She

   _____ Spanish because the

   Spanish teacher _____ sick all semester.

4. A. _____ you speak to Jennifer yesterday?

   B. No, I _____ . I _____

   to her husband. Jennifer _____ there when I called.

5. A. _____ Louise eat her dinner last night?

   B. Yes, she _____ . She _____ so

   hungry that she _____ three hamburgers.

6. A. Did your children _____ up on time this morning?

   B. No, they _____ . They

   _____ so tired that they got up at noon.

C. Write the question.

Ex. We're arguing with <u>our neighbors</u>.

   _____ *Who are you arguing with?* _____

1. I'm writing about <u>my favorite book</u>.

   _____

2. They're going to call <u>the landlord</u>.

   _____

3. She swam <u>in the ocean</u>.

   _____

4. He'll be ready <u>in a few minutes</u>.

   _____

5. They came <u>by boat</u>.

   _____

6. She's going to take <u>five</u> photographs.

   _____

7. We'll be staying in London <u>until Tuesday</u>.

   _____

D. Answer the questions.

Ex. What did Tom do yesterday morning?

(ride his bicycle) _____ *He rode his bicycle.* _____

1. What's Nancy doing today?

   (visit her neighbors) _____

2. What does Jim do every afternoon?

   (watch TV) _____

3. What are you and your friends doing today?

   (have a party) _____

4. What did Roger and Jack do yesterday afternoon?

   (go bowling) _____

5. What was Dan doing when his wife came home?

   (bake bread) _____

6. What are you going to do tomorrow?

   (clean my apartment) _____

7. What will you and your husband be doing this evening?

   (play cards) _____

8. How will your daughter get to school tomorrow if it snows?

   (take the bus) _____

E. Listen to each question and then complete the answer.

Ex. Yes, _____*she does*_____ .

1. Yes, _____ .   5. No, _____ .

2. Yes, _____ .   6. Yes, _____ .

3. No, _____ .   7. No, _____ .

4. Yes, _____ .   8. No, _____ .

A. NOT TODAY

1. Donald isn't going to go to the beach today.

   _He's_ already _gone_ to the beach this week.

   He went to the beach yesterday.

2. I'm not going to write to my granddaughter today.

   _____ already _____ to her this week.

   _____ to her on Monday.

3. Shirley isn't going to eat any pizza tonight.

   _____ already _____ pizza this week.

   _____ pizza on Friday.

4. We aren't going to do our laundry today.

   _____ already _____ our laundry this week.

   _____ our laundry yesterday.

5. Ted isn't going to wear his black suit today.

   _____ already _____ his black suit this week.

   _____ it on Saturday.

6. Alan and Irene aren't going to take a violin lesson today.

   _____ already _____ a violin lesson this week.

   _____ a violin lesson on Tuesday.

(continued)

7. Frank isn't going to give his girlfriend flowers tonight.

_____ already _____ her flowers this week.

_____ her flowers on Sunday.

8. We aren't going to spend a lot of money at the store today.

_____ already _____ a lot of money at the store this week.

_____ a lot of money yesterday.

9. I'm not going to buy any tomatoes today.

_____ already _____ a lot of tomatoes this week.

_____ a dozen tomatoes on Thursday.

10. Mary isn't going to swim today.

_____ already _____ this week.

_____ on Saturday.

11. Sam isn't going to cook French food today.

_____ already _____ French food this week.

_____ French food on Wednesday.

12. Henry and Walter aren't going to go bowling today.

_____ already _____ bowling this week.

_____ bowling on Tuesday.

B. WHAT ARE THEY SAYING?

1. A. Peggy, you've got to take a bath.

   B. But, Mother, ___*I've*___ already _____ a bath today.

   A. Really? When?

   B. Don't you remember? _____ a bath this morning.

2. A. Would you like to see a movie today?

   B. I don't think so. _____ already _____ a movie this week.

   A. Really? When?

   B. _____ a movie on Monday.

3. A. Are you going on vacation soon?

   B. No. _____ already _____ on vacation.

   A. Oh, that's right. I forgot. _____ on vacation last January.

4. A. I hope Timmy gets a haircut soon.

   B. Don't worry, Mother. _____ already _____ one.

   A. I'm glad to hear that. When?

   B. _____ a haircut yesterday.

   A. That's wonderful.

C. IN A LONG TIME

clean	eat	go	read	study
dance	fix	have	see	take
do		practice		write

1. Rover looks hungry. He _hasn't eaten_ anything in a long time.

2. I'm very sorry, but I _____ _____ in a long time.

3. I really think Johnny should go to school today. He _____ to school in a long time.

4. What's the matter, Theodore? You aren't playing very well.

I know. I _____ in a long time.

5. Marylou's room is very dirty.

I know. She _____ it in a long time.

6. I'm really excited. I'm going to see my grandmother today. I _____ _____ her in a long time.

7. All my clothes are dirty. I don't have anything to wear.

I know. I _____ the laundry in a long time.

8. The landlord says he's going to fix our washing machine today.

I don't believe it. He _____ _____ anything in our apartment in a long time.

9. When are you going to take me to a baseball game? You _____ _____ me to one in a long time.

10. I think Charlie watches too much TV. He _____ a book in a long time.

11. Who was the sixteenth president of the United States?

I can't remember. I _____ _____ American history in a long time.

12. I hope Carol and Arthur are okay. They _____ to us in a long time.

13. We _____ a quiet evening together in a long time.

D. WHAT ARE THEY SAYING?

1. _Have_ you _gone_ to the post office yet?

   Yes, _I have_. I went there this morning.

2. _____ Kathy _____ to you yet?

   Yes, _____. She wrote to me last week.

3. _____ you and Alan _____ the play at the Grant Theater yet?

   Yes, _____. We saw it last night.

4. _____ Robert _____ his new tuxedo yet?

   Yes, _____. He wore it last Sunday.

5. _____ your parents _____ you to the new candy store yet?

   Yes, _____. They took me there yesterday.

6. _____ you and your wife _____ any plans for the summer yet?

   Yes, _____. We made them last week.

7. _____ Susan _____ your parents yet?

   Yes, _____. She met them last weekend.

8. _____ you _____ your homework yet?

   Yes, _____. I did it this afternoon.

9. _____ Sharon and Charles _____ home yet?

   Yes, _____. They got home a few minutes ago.

10. _____ you _____ Henry his birthday present yet?

    Yes, _____. I gave it to him this morning.

11. _____ Norman _____ his new motorcycle yet?

    Yes, _____. He rode it this afternoon.

E. A LOT OF THINGS TO DO

William is going to have a party tonight,
and he has a lot of things to do.

✓	go shopping
	clean my apartment
	get a haircut
✓	bake bread
	make dessert
✓	fix the stereo

1. _____*He's already gone shopping.*_____

2. _____*He hasn't cleaned his apartment yet.*_____

3. _____

4. _____

5. _____

6. _____

Tom and Lucy are going on
vacation tomorrow, and they have
a lot of things to do.

	do our laundry
✓	pay our electric bill
	pack our suitcases
✓	return our library books
✓	buy a new tennis racket
	say good-bye to our neighbors

7. _____

8. _____

9. _____

10. _____

11. _____

12. _____

(continued)

Jane has a lot of work to do at the office today.

☑	write to Mrs. Peters
☐	call Miss Watson
☑	take Mr. Warren to lunch
☐	meet with Mr. Grant
☑	send income tax forms to the new employees
☐	fire Mr. Smith

13. _____

14. _____

15. _____

16. _____

17. _____

18. _____

You have a lot of things to do today.
What have you already done?
What haven't you done yet?

1. ....

2. ....

3. ....

4. ....

5. ....

6. ....

F. IS OR HAS?

1. He's already eaten dinner.

   _____ is

   ___✓___ has

2. He's eating dinner.

   ___✓___ is

   _____ has

3. She's washing her car.

   _____ is

   _____ has

4. She's given us a lot of homework this week.

   _____ is

   _____ has

5. He's having a terrible time.

   _____ is

   _____ has

6. She's going to leave.

   _____ is

   _____ has

7. He's bought a lot of clothes recently.

   _____ is

   _____ has

8. It's raining.

   _____ is

   _____ has

9. She's hungry.

   _____ is

   _____ has

10. He's got to study.

    _____ is

    _____ has

11. Where's the nearest restaurant?

    _____ is

    has

12. She's written to her family.

    _____ is

    _____ has

13. He's taking a lot of photographs.

    _____ is

    _____ has

14. He's taken a few photographs.

    _____ is

    _____ has

15. He's spent all his money.

    _____ is

    _____ has

16. There's a laundromat across the street.

    _____ is

    _____ has

17. She's gone shopping.

    _____ is

    _____ has

18. It's very cold.

    _____ is

    _____ has

19. He's embarrassed.

    _____ is

    _____ has

20. This is the best science fiction book she's ever read.

    _____ is

    _____ has

G. WHAT ARE THEY SAYING?

1. A. I'm upset. I ___*wrote*___ a letter to Mary last month, and she _____

   _____ back yet.

   B. Don't worry. I'm sure _____ write to you soon.

2. A. _____ you seen Arthur's new motorcycle yet?

   B. No, _____. When _____ he get it?

   A. He _____ it yesterday, and _____ already ridden it everywhere.

   He _____ it to my house yesterday afternoon.

3. A. Have you _____ any good movies recently?

   B. No, I _____. I _____ a movie a week ago, but it was terrible.

   A. Really? What movie did _____?

   B. "The Magnificent Monkey." It's one of the worst movies I've ever _____.

4. A. _____ you spoken to Donald recently?

   B. Yes, _____. I _____ to him yesterday.

   A. What _____ he say?

   B. He's worried because he _____ done his English homework in a long time, and his

   teacher is _____ give an English test tomorrow.

42

5. A. What _____ you get for your birthday yesterday?

    B. My parents _____ me fifty dollars.

    A. That's great!   What _____?

    B. Going to buy?   I've already _____ all my birthday money.

    A. Really?   What _____ buy?

    B. I _____ two videocassettes.   Would you like to see them?

6. A. Are you ready to leave?

    B. No, _____.   I haven't _____ a bath yet.

    A. I don't believe it!   You _____ up an hour ago.   You're really slow today.   _____ you eaten breakfast yet?

    B. Of course, _____.   I _____ a little while ago, and I've already _____ the dishes.

    A. Well, hurry up!   It's 8:30, and I don't want to be late.

 H. LISTEN

Listen to each word and then say it.

{j!}

1. jacket
2. January
3. jelly
4. Jimmy
5. jogging
6. journalist
7. just
8. pajamas

{y!}

1. yard
2. year
3. yellow
4. yesterday
5. yet
6. yogurt
7. young
8. New York

I. __ULIA'S BROKEN T__PEWRITER

Julia's typewriter is broken. The j's and the y's don't always work. Fill in the missing j's and y's, and then read Julia's letters aloud.

1.
> J udy,
>   Did I leave my blue and Y ellow __acket at __our house __esterday after the __azz concert? I __ust can't find it anywhere.
>   __ulia

2.
> Dear __ennifer,
>   We're sorry __ou and __oe can't visit us this __une. Do __ou think __ou can come in __uly? We really en__oyed __our visit last __ear.
>   __ulia

3.
> __eff,
>   __ack and I are out __ogging, but we'll be back in __ust a few minutes. Make __ourself comfortable. __ou can wait for us in the __ard. If __ou're thirsty, take some __uice from the refrigerator.
>   __ulia

4.
> Dear __ane,
>   Thank __ou very much for the beautiful pa__amas you sent __immy. He received them __esterday. __immy is too __oung to write to __ou himself, but he says, "Thank __ou." I'm sure he'll en__oy wearing his new pa__amas on cold __anuary nights.
>   Love,
>   __ulia

5.
> __ack,
>   We need a __ar of __elly, a large can of orange __uice, and some __ogurt. Would __ou please buy them when __ou go to the store today?
>   __ulia

6.
> Dear __anet,
>   We got a letter from George __ackson __ust last week. He's really en__oying college this __ear. His favorite sub__ects are German and __apanese. He's looking for a __ob in New __ork as a __ournalist, but he hasn't found one __et.
>   __ulia

A. HOW LONG?

for	since

1.

How long have you had a toothache?

I've had a toothache _for_ three days.

2. A. How long have you played the violin?

   B. _____ 1985.

3. A. How long have your parents lived in London?

   B. _____ a long time.

4. A. How long has Betsy been interested in boys?

   B. _____ several months.

5. A. How long has Mr. Morgan been an electrician?

   B. _____ 1963.

6. A. How long have you and Jennifer known each other?

   B. _____ ten years.

7. A. How long have your neighbors been in Europe?

   B. _____ February.

8. A. How long have you had problems with your landlord?

   B. _____ a year.

9. A. How long has Hilda liked science fiction books?

   B. _____ last year.

10. A. How long has your grandmother owned her own motorcycle?

    B. _____ 1965.

11.

How long have there been mice in your apartment?

_____

_____ two months!

B. WHAT'S THE QUESTION?

1. _____ *How long has* _____ Steve _____ *wanted to be a doctor* _____ ?
   He's wanted to be a doctor for a long time.

2. _____ Lucy _____ ?
   She's owned her own car since 1986.

3. _____ your parents _____ ?
   They've been married for 25 years.

4. _____ you _____ ?
   I've been interested in computer technology since last year.

5. _____ Alan _____ ?
   He's worn glasses for six years.

6. _____ you and your boyfriend _____ ?
   We've been angry at each other for a week.

7. _____ your sisters _____ ?
   They've known how to knit for many years.

8. _____ your daughter _____ ?
   She's had a boyfriend for several months.

9. _____ there _____ ?
   There's been a health club in town since last winter.

46

C. SINCE WHEN?

1. ___I'm___ very tired today.

   ___I've been___ tired since I got up this morning.

2. Nancy _____ very well.

   _____ very well since she was six years old.

3. _____ lost.

   _____ lost since we arrived here four hours ago.

4. _____ cloudy.

   _____ cloudy since last week.

5. _____ nervous.

   _____ nervous since I got married a few hours ago.

6. Fred _____ very hard.

   _____ hard since he came here two months ago.

7. My kitchen sink _____ broken.

   _____ broken since yesterday morning.

(continued)   47

8. My neighbors _____ every night.

   _____ every night since they moved here last month.

9. My sister _____ the violin very well.

   _____ very well since she was four years old.

10. My children and I _____ very cold.

    _____ cold since the radiator broke two hours ago.

11. I _____ a backache.

    _____ a backache since I played basketball with my son this morning.

12. My boyfriend _____ bored.

    _____ bored since this movie started three hours ago.

13. My feet _____ .

    _____ since I hiked ten miles last weekend.

D. SCRAMBLED SENTENCES

Unscramble the sentences.

1. last   had   Helen   a   night   headache   has   since

   _____

2. he   little   the   since   played   a   boy   he's   violin   was

   _____

3. history   I've   in   I   Greek   interested   since   Athens   been   visited

   _____

4. since   Paul   been   they   and   college   Sara   engaged   have   finished

   _____

5. piano   how   since   we've   young   to   the   known   play   very   were   we

   _____

6. professional   she   wanted   a   to   musician   ten   she's   years   since   old   be   was

   _____

7. business   their   they've   they   computer   started   owned   personal   a   since   own

   _____

E. WRITE ABOUT YOURSELF

1. I'm interested in ....

   I've been interested in .... since ....

2. I like ....

   I've .... since ....

3. I want to ....

   I've .... since ....

4. I know how to ....

   I've .... since ....

F. THEN AND NOW

go	like	teach
have	live	visit

1. Mr. and Mrs. Grant ___go___ to the

   symphony every week. _____

   _____ to the symphony every week since
   they moved to the city. Before that,

   _____ never _____ to the
   symphony. They stayed home and listened
   to records.

2. Before she moved to Mexico, Professor Wilson

   _____ French. Now _____

   _____ Spanish. _____

   _____ Spanish at a Mexican
   university for the past three years.

3. I _____ in an apartment since
   1987. Before I got my own apartment,

   _____ with my
   parents.

4. Henry doesn't like rock music any more.

   _____ it when he was in

   high school, but now _____

   jazz. _____ jazz for many years.

5. Your Aunt Gertrude _____ already

   _____ us five times this year!

   Last year, she _____ us only twice.

   How many times will she _____ us
   next year?!

6. Nelson _____ a lot of gray hair now.

   _____ a lot of gray hair since
   he started to teach English five years ago.

   Before that, _____ black hair.
   We all think he worries too much!

G. LOOKING BACK

Ralph
carpenter 1970–now
electrician 1955–1969

1. How long _____*has Ralph been*_____ a carpenter?

   _____ *He's been a carpenter* since *1970* .

2. How long _____*was he*_____ an electrician?

   _____ for _____ .

Mrs. Watson
English teacher 1980–now
German teacher 1971–1979

3. How long _____ an English teacher?

   _____ for _____ .

4. How long _____ a German teacher?

   _____ for _____ .

my grandparents
Democrats   1973–now
Republicans 1930–1973

5. How long _____ Republicans?

   _____ for _____ .

6. How long _____ Democrats?

   _____ since _____ .

Maria
(work)
bank   1985–now
post office   1974–1985

7. How long _____ at the bank?

   _____ since _____ .

8. How long _____ at the post office?

   _____ for _____ .

Bob and Betsy
(live)
Madrid   1987–now
Toronto   1975–1987

9. How long _____ in Toronto?

   _____ for _____ .

10. How long _____ in Madrid?

    _____ since _____ .

H. HIGH SCHOOL REUNION

CLASS REUNION

1. Do you still go dancing every weekend.

No. ....
.... (for/since) ....
....

2. Do you still lift weights every morning?

No. ....
.... (for/since) ....

3. Are you still a Republican?

No. ....
.... (for/since) ....
....

4. How long have you been interested in
....?
....
.... (for/since) ....
....

I. LISTEN: *The Baker Family*

Listen to the story and fill in the information. Then use the information to answer the questions below.

Mr. Baker

    1. math teacher: for _____

    2. before that: _____

Mrs. Baker

    3. professional violinist: since _____

    4. symphonies: _____

Jeff

    5. sports car driver: for _____

    6. computers: since _____

Nancy

    7. winter sports: since _____

    8. ski: for _____

Charlie

    9. count to a hundred: since _____

    10. play the violin: for _____

Listen and answer each question in a complete sentence.

    1. _____

    2. _____

    3. _____

    4. _____

    5. _____

    6. _____

    7. _____

    8. _____

    9. _____

    10. _____

A. HOW LONG?

1. How long has Bill been sleeping?

   He's been sleeping since
   10:00 last night.

2. How long have Bill and Mary been watching TV?

   _____
   several hours.

3. How long has Betsy been making her own clothes?

   _____
   she got married.

4. How long have we been jogging?

   _____
   ten minutes.

5. How long has Professor Jones been talking?

   _____
   two hours.

6. How long have Louise and Jeffrey been dancing?

   _____
   the party began.

7. How long have you been teaching?

   _____
   1950.

8. How long have I been lying here?

   _____
   a week.

(continued)

9. How long has Marylou been studying?

_____

early this morning.

10. How long have you and your wife been skating?

_____

three hours.

11. How long have Mr. and Mrs. Baker been doing aerobics?

_____

a half hour.

12. How long has Billy been crying?

_____

his sister ate his ice cream.

B. WHAT ARE THEY DOING?

1. (read)   Tom _____*is reading*_____ .

         _____*He's been reading*_____ since noon.

2. (work)   Mrs. Thompson _____ .

         _____ since early this morning.

3. (bake)   My sister and I _____ cookies.

         _____ cookies for several hours.

4. (ride)   Steve _____ his bicycle.

         _____ his bicycle since 3:00.

5. (fight)   You and your brother _____ .

         _____ all morning.

6. (write)   Shirley _____ her English composition.

         _____ her English composition for an hour.

7. (take care of)   Fred _____ his little brother.

         _____ his little brother since 6:00.

8. (complain)   My parents _____ .

         _____ since I broke the living room window this morning.

C. SOUND IT OUT

Listen to each word and then say it.

<u>this</u>:
1. w<u>i</u>nter
2. dent<u>i</u>st
3. ch<u>i</u>cken
4. l<u>i</u>ft
5. b<u>ui</u>lding
6. <u>i</u>tself

<u>these</u>:
1. agr<u>ee</u>
2. sp<u>ea</u>k
3. br<u>ie</u>fcase
4. arm<u>y</u>
5. f<u>e</u>ver
6. <u>ea</u>ten

Listen and put a circle around the word that has the same sound.

1. s<u>i</u>ck: pol<u>i</u>ce   t<u>i</u>red   (h<u>i</u>s)
2. teenager: h<u>ea</u>dache   t<u>ea</u>cher   sw<u>ea</u>ter
3. s<u>ee</u>n: P<u>e</u>ter   b<u>ee</u>n   fl<u>y</u>
4. h<u>i</u>mself: w<u>i</u>ll   dec<u>i</u>de   tax<u>i</u>
5. asl<u>ee</u>p: m<u>e</u>t   <u>e</u>vening   clin<u>i</u>c
6. f<u>i</u>shing: sc<u>i</u>ence   wr<u>i</u>ting   h<u>i</u>story
7. l<u>ea</u>ve: s<u>ee</u>ing   h<u>ea</u>vy   w<u>i</u>nter
8. m<u>i</u>lk: h<u>i</u>re   s<u>i</u>dewalk   th<u>i</u>s
9. ch<u>ea</u>p: tr<u>i</u>p   b<u>e</u>   <u>i</u>nterested

Now make a sentence using all the words you circled. Read the sentence aloud.

10. _____ _____ _____ _____ _____ _____ _____ _____

11. g<u>i</u>ven: <u>ea</u>sy   <u>i</u>sn't   dr<u>i</u>ving'
12. betw<u>ee</u>n: d<u>i</u>nner   beg<u>i</u>n   h<u>e</u>'ll
13. <u>i</u>nterview: b<u>i</u>cycle   th<u>i</u>s   <u>i</u>ron
14. tenn<u>i</u>s: b<u>u</u>sy   th<u>e</u>se   p<u>ie</u>ce
15. angr<u>y</u>:   t<u>y</u>pe   v<u>i</u>olin   w<u>ee</u>kend
16. people: L<u>i</u>nda   G<u>i</u>nger   St<u>e</u>ve
17. tr<u>i</u>ck: Gr<u>ee</u>k   <u>i</u>f   ch<u>i</u>ld
18. w<u>i</u>sh: v<u>i</u>sit   sl<u>i</u>ce   athl<u>e</u>te
19. y<u>ea</u>r: w<u>ea</u>r   m<u>e</u>   h<u>ea</u>rt

Now make a sentence using all the words you circled. Read the sentence aloud.

20. _____ _____ _____ _____ _____ _____ _____ _____ _____

D. WHAT ARE THEY SAYING?

cry	rain	wait
live	smoke	wear
play	study	work

1. Mrs. Harris, please come home soon. The baby is crying, and I don't know what to do.

_____Has he been crying_____ for a long time?

Yes, he _____. _____ all evening.

2. My doctor says I should stop smoking, but I don't think I'll be able to.

_____ for a long time?

Yes, I _____. _____ for more than twenty years.

3. I'm sorry I'm late. _____ for a long time?

No, I _____. I just got here a few minutes ago.

4. Have you met our new secretary, Ms. Clark, yet?

No, I _____. How long _____ _____ here?

_____ here for three days.

5. What a terrible day! _____ _____ for a long time?

Yes, it _____. _____ since 5:00 this morning.

6. _____ in Centerville for a long time?

No, _____. I just moved here last week.

7.

> Your son and daughter speak English very well. _____ it for a long time?

> Yes, they _____ . _____ English for five years.

8.

> Your shirt is very dirty. _____ it all week?

> No, _____ . I just put it on this morning.

9.

> This is the tenth chess game you've won today. _____ for a long time?

> No, I _____ . _____ for only a few months.

> Really? I don't believe it.

E. YOU DECIDE: *What Have They Been Doing?*

1. I have a sore throat.

No wonder you have a sore throat! ....*You've been singing* (or)..........

..........................*You've been talking*.......................... all day.

2. Sally and Andy can't finish their dinner.

No wonder they can't finish their dinner! ....

.... all day.

3. My feet hurt.

No wonder your feet hurt! ....

.... all day.

4. Carl has a headache.

No wonder he has a headache! ....

.... all day.

5. David doesn't have any money.

No wonder he doesn't have any money! ....

.... all week.

6. George and his wife are depressed.

No wonder they're depressed! ....

.... all day.

7. Julie looks very healthy.

No wonder she looks healthy! ....

.... all summer.

59

F. WHAT'S HAPPENING?

drink	listen	play	swim
eat	meet	read	talk
give	paint	study	type

1. My son and daughter are very tired. _____*They've been studying*_____

   since they got home from school. ___*They've*___ already ___*studied*___

   French, English, and history. They won't be able to go to sleep until

   very late tonight. _____ mathematics yet.

2. Sally is exhausted. _____ her apartment since

   10:00 this morning. _____ already _____ the bathroom,

   the living room, and the kitchen. And she isn't finished. _____

   _____ her bedroom yet!

3. Mr. Arnold is enjoying himself. _____

   since noon. _____ already _____ six short stories.

4. My husband and I are very full. _____ for the

   last two hours. _____ already _____ a lot of soup,

   salad, chicken, and potatoes. And our dinner isn't finished. _____

   _____ our dessert yet!

5. Steve is very thirsty. _____

   lemonade all day. _____ already _____ eight glasses.

6. Frieda is getting tired. _____ for an

   hour. _____ already _____ across the pool twenty times.

60

7. Mr. and Mrs. Anderson are enjoying themselves. _____

_____ cards since 5:00 this evening.

_____ already _____ ten games, and they

_____ lost one yet.

8. I'm having a wonderful time. _____

to music all morning. _____ already _____ to all my

favorite records.

9. Sarah is really tired. _____ since she

got to work. _____ already _____ 15 letters.

10. Mr. and Mrs. Grant love to talk. _____ all

evening. _____ already _____ about their family,

their friends, and their vacation. (Fortunately, _____

_____ about their pet bird yet!)

11. I'm having a busy day. _____ with my

employees since 8:00 this morning. _____ already

_____ with 20 employees.

12. Professor Hawkins is really exhausted today. _____

lectures since 9:00 this morning. _____ already _____ two

lectures, and he has to give another one in a few minutes.

G. A NEW LIFE

Toshi has been living in a small town in Japan all his life. His father just got a job in the United States, and Toshi and his family are going to live there. Toshi's life is going to be very different in the United States.

1. He's going to live in a big city.
2. He's going to take English lessons.
3. He's going to shop in American supermarkets.
4. He's going to eat American food.
5. He's going to ....

Toshi is a little nervous.

1. _____*He's never lived in a big city*_____ before.

2. _____ before.

3. _____ before.

4. _____ before.

5. .... before.

Toshi's cousins have been living in the United States for many years. They'll be able to help him.

1. _____*They've been living in a big city*_____ for years.

2. _____ for years.

3. _____ for years.

4. _____ for years.

5. .... for years.

Toshi's cousins tell him he shouldn't worry. They're sure he'll enjoy his new life in the United States very much.

H. YOU DECIDE: *A New Life*

.... has been living in .... all her life.   Now she's

going to move to ....   Her life is going to be very different in
(your city)

....
(your city)

1. She's going to ....

2. She's going to ....

3. She's going to ....

4. She's going to ....

5. She's going to ....

_____ is a little nervous.

1. She's never _____ before.

2. She's never _____ before.

3. She's never _____ before.

4. She's never _____ before.

5. She's never _____ before.

.... (has/have) been living in _____ for many
years and will be able to help her.

1. _____ for years.

2. _____ for years.

3. _____ for years.

4. _____ for years.

5. _____ for years.

_____ shouldn't worry.   I'm sure she'll enjoy her new life in _____
very much.

I. YOU DECIDE: *Asking for a Raise*

A. Mr. Harris. Could I speak with you for a few minutes?

B. Of course. Please sit down.

A. Mr. Harris, I've been thinking. I've been working here at the ....
Company (for/since) .... I've worked very hard, and I've done a lot of
things here. For example, I've ...., I've ....
...., and I've been .... (for/since)
....

B. That's true, Mr. Jones. And we're happy with your work.

A. Thank you, Mr. Harris. As I was saying, I know I've done a very good job here and I really
think I should get a raise. I haven't had a raise (for/since) ....
....

B. ....
....
....

A. ....
....
....

J. LISTEN

Listen and fill in the missing words.

1. I've been _____ a lot of _____ recently, but I _____ _____ any
   that I've really liked. What good movies _____ you _____ _____ month? _____
   you _____ _____ any movies _____ _____?

2. Ted _____ _____ _____ very long, but he _____ whenever
   he _____. _____ already _____ downtown three times _____
   _____ , and I think _____ _____ downtown again this afternoon.

3. Sheila _____ _____ a _____ _____ photographs of her _____.
   _____ _____ _____ photographs of _____ for _____. I think_____
   _____ photographs are the _____ ones _____ _____ _____.

4. Mrs. Warren _____ _____ _____ piano lessons this _____ , and
   _____ _____ another lesson _____ a _____ _____. After
   that, _____ _____ _____ _____ any more lessons _____.

5. Bobby _____ _____ his dinner tonight because _____ already _____
   dessert. Bobby _____ _____ _____ very well _____ his grandmother
   _____ _____ a large box of _____ _____ week.

CHECK-UP TEST: *Chapters 4–6*

A. Complete the sentences with the present perfect.

Ex. (do)   Stuart __*has*__ already __*done*__ his homework.

    (read)   I __*haven't read*__ the newspaper yet.

(go)   1.   Max and his brother _____ already _____ to the beach.

(take)   2.   Diane _____ her piano lesson yet.

(write) 3. I _____ to my parents yet.

(eat) 4. My wife and I _____ already _____ dinner.

(pay) 5. You _____ your electric bill yet.

(leave) 6. Herbert _____ already _____ for work.

B. Complete the questions.

1. _____ her new necklace yet?

    Yes, she has. She wore it yesterday.

2. _____ home yet?

    Yes, they have. They got home a little while ago.

3. _____ to the doctor yet?

    No, I haven't. I'm going to speak to her this afternoon.

4. _____ the new movie at the Central Theater yet?

    Yes, he has. He saw it last week.

5. _____ ever _____ in a marathon?

    Yes, I have. I ran in a marathon last spring.

6. _____ ever _____ in an airplane?

    Yes, she has. She flew to Madrid two years ago.

C. Complete the sentences.

Ex. I'm very tired. _____*I've been*_____ tired since I got up this morning.

    Susan is reading. _____*She's been reading*_____ since noon.

1. It's cloudy. _____ cloudy since yesterday.

2. We're studying. _____ since 3:00.

3. My son has a toothache. _____ a toothache since early this morning.

4. My children are arguing. _____ all morning.

5. Jane is sleeping. _____ since 8:00 last night.

6. My sister and I are interested in Italian art. _____ interested in Italian art since we visited Rome.

7. I'm baking cookies. _____ cookies for several hours.

8. Richard knows how to ski. _____ how to ski since he was very young.

D. Complete the answers.

> for   since

1. How long has your father been working at the post office?

    _____ 1975.

2. How long has your daughter been married?

    _____ three years.

3. How long have you and your friend been waiting?

    _____ an hour.

4. How long has it been raining?

    _____ Friday.

5. How long have you wanted to be an actress?

    _____ I was a teenager.

E. Complete the sentences.

1. Ted owns a car. _____ a car since last year.

    Before that, _____ a motorcycle.

2. I'm a mechanic. _____ a mechanic since 1980.

    Before that, _____ a plumber.

3. My neighbors have a cat. _____ a cat since last winter.

    Before that, _____ a dog.

4. My daughter likes jazz. _____ jazz for the past few months.

    Before that, _____ rock music.

F. Listen and fill in the missing words.

1. A. Timothy _____ _____ _____ since _____ _____ up. _____
                    1   2   3   4   5   6
    already _____ more than ten pages. Who's he _____ _____?
             7   8   9
    B. He's probably _____ to _____ girlfriend. He _____ _____ to _____
                        10   11   12   13   14
    _____ weeks.
      15

2. Mrs. Morgan _____ _____ three violin lessons this _____, but she _____
                  16   17   18   19
    _____ _____ any more lessons this afternoon. She's _____ _____
      20   21   22   23
    a lot of lessons _____, and she's _____ tired.
                       24   25

67

A. WHAT DO THEY { ENJOY DOING / LIKE TO DO }?

| enjoy _____ ing | _____ ing |
| like to _____ | |

1. I don't enjoy _____*going*_____ to the doctor, but I went yesterday for my annual checkup.

2. Mrs. McDonald is very energetic. She _____*likes to*_____ lift weights. She thinks that

   _____*lifting*_____ weights is good exercise.

3. William _____ baking bread when he has free time.

4. I _____ swim after a busy day. In my opinion, _____ is a good way to relax.

5. My husband doesn't _____ working late at the office, but sometimes he has to.

6. My wife and I ski during the winter, and in the summer we _____ to play tennis.

7. Bob doesn't _____ give blood, but he knows that _____ blood is a good thing to do.

8. Roberta doesn't _____ lying in the sun because she's afraid she'll get a sunburn.

9. My wife _____ jog five miles every day. She thinks _____ is the best exercise in the world.

10. I _____ go to parties. I think _____ is a good way to meet people.

11. School is okay, but my brother and I don't really _____ doing homework.

12. Alice _____ eat rich desserts, but her doctor thinks that _____ rich desserts is bad for her heart.

13. Mary doesn't really enjoy _____ her apartment, but she tries to clean it once a week.

14. My little brother doesn't _____ go to bed at eight o'clock. He thinks _____ to bed at eight o'clock is too early.

15. My husband and I get up early during the week, but on weekends we enjoy _____ late.

16. I really want to learn English, but I don't _____ study.

68

B. YOU DECIDE: *What's the Reason?*

1. Fred is happy he works in a restaurant because he enjoys .... *baking fancy desserts* (or)

.... *eating lots of good food* (or) cooking different kinds of foods.

2. Andy hates living in the city because he can't stand ....

....

3. Mr. Davis is glad he's a teacher because he likes ....

....

4. I'm sorry I'm a secretary because I can't stand ....

....

5. Michael is glad he's going to college next year because he enjoys ....

....

6. Martin enjoys living in Honolulu because he likes ....

....

7. Diane wants to be a carpenter because she enjoys ....

....

8. Mrs. Watson is sorry she has ten children because she hates ....

....

9. Gloria is very happy she's a Hollywood actress because she enjoys ....

....

10. Marion is glad she knows how to speak English because she likes ....

....

C. MY ENERGETIC GRANDMOTHER

A. Your grandmother is a very energetic woman.

B. She sure is!

A. When did she start _____ tennis?
   ₁

B. Believe it or not, she learned _____ tennis when she was sixty years old!
   ₂

A. That's fantastic!   Does she _____ tennis often?
₃

B. Yes, she does.   She plays every day.

A. What else does she enjoy doing?

B. She enjoys ...., she enjoys ....,
4   5

and she also enjoys ....
6

A. I hope I have that much energy when I'm her age!

D. I CAN'T STAND IT!

I spoke to my friend Roberta last weekend, and she talked a lot about tap dancing.   Ever since she started to tap dance a few months ago, that's all she ever talks about!   I never see her anymore because she practices tap dancing all the time.   And whenever I talk to her on the phone, tap dancing is the only thing she wants to talk about!   (She thinks that everybody should learn to tap dance.)
I can't stand it!   I don't ever want to hear another word about tap dancing!

Now YOU tell about somebody.

I spoke to my friend .... last weekend, and .... talked a lot about

....   Ever since ....

....

....

....

....

....

....

....

70

E. YOU DECIDE: *What's Lucy Going to Do?*

A. Hello, Lucy.   How are you?   I haven't seen you in a long time.   Tell me, what have you been doing?

B. ....

A. Oh.   And what have you decided to do after you finish studying English?

B. I've decided ....

A. Really?   You're going to move to the United States?   That's wonderful!   What are you going to do there?

B. I'm considering ....

....

A. Don't you think that .... will be difficult?

B. Oh, no.   Not at all.

A. Have you considered ....?

B. Yes, I have.   But I've decided not to because ....

....

....

A. And where have you decided to live?

B. I'm thinking about ....

A. Why do you want to live there?

B. ....

....

A. Well, Lucy.   Good luck.   Let's get together sometime before you leave.

B. Okay.   Good-bye.

A. Good-bye.

F. PROBLEMS

1. I'm very worried about my son. He keeps on ___*eating*___ junk food. I tell him that junk food is bad for his teeth, but

   he doesn't listen to me. He really should begin _____ more fruits and vegetables.

2. Linda speaks so softly in class. She really should begin

   _____ louder. No one can hear her at all.

3. If my neighbor's son doesn't stop _____ his violin at four o'clock in the morning, I'm going to have to complain to the landlord. He really should start

   _____ his violin during the day.

4. Maybe I shouldn't continue _____ basketball twice a day. I really like basketball, but I'm afraid I might hurt my back if I keep on

   _____ so often.

5. I've got to stop _____ late at the office

   every night. If I don't quit _____ late,

   my family will start _____ angry at me.

6. I'm really upset. My sister started _____ me early this morning, and she hasn't stopped. If

   she keeps on _____ me, I'm going to cry. And I

   won't stop _____ until she stops _____ me!

72

7. Do you think I should continue _____
English? I'm not a very good student. My friends

tell me I should keep on _____
English. According to them, if I quit

_____ English now, I won't be able to
speak it when I travel.

8. Harvey has got to stop _____ so fast and

start _____ more carefully. _____
fast isn't safe.

9. Mr. Smith! When are you going to begin _____

_____ more neatly? If you don't stop _____
so sloppily, I'm going to have to fire you.

10. My boyfriend George is so clumsy. When we go

dancing, he keeps on _____ on my
feet. I like to dance with him, but if he doesn't

stop _____ on my feet, I'm never going
to dance with him again.

11. I should quit _____ scary TV programs

before I go to bed. If I keep on _____

scary TV programs, I'll keep on _____
nightmares.

12. Should I stop _____ out with Doris and start

_____ out with Jane? Or should I keep on

_____ out with Doris and go out with Jane,
too? I really can't decide because I like them both!

Listen and put a circle around the correct answer.

1. a. listen to jazz.
   b. (going to the symphony.)

2. a. eating junk food.
   b. to pay our bills late.

3. a. to sew.
   b. baking bread.

4. a. to ski.
   b. figure skating.

5. a. to buy a new TV.
   b. taking a vacation.

6. a. moving to my own apartment.
   b. to ask for a raise.

7. a. to go back to college?
   b. finding a new job?

8. a. to eat candy.
   b. having so much ice cream.

9. a. making mistakes?
   b. to go to bed after midnight?

10. a. to worry so much.
    b. smoking.

11. a. get a good night's sleep.
    b. playing chess.

12. a. going to the dentist.
    b. see the doctor.

13. a. taking violin lessons?
    b. study the piano?

14. a. to do his history homework.
    b. clean his apartment.

15. a. studying astronomy.
    b. teach a computer course.

16. a. to live at home with your parents.
    b. going to school for the rest of your life.

H. WHAT DOES IT MEAN?

Put a circle around the correct answer.

1. Harry is going to the health club this afternoon.
   a. He has a doctor's appointment.
   b. (He's going to exercise.)
   c. He's going to have a checkup.

2. Peter and Helen are engaged.
   a. They don't know each other.
   b. They're married.
   c. They're going to get married.

3. My wife has a fever.
   a. I'm glad to hear that.
   b. How long has she been feeling sick?
   c. Do you think I can borrow it?

4. Carmen has made plans for the summer.

    a. She knows what she's going to do this summer.

    b. She hasn't decided what she's going to do this summer.

    c. She's made a lot of new summer clothes.

5. What's your present address?

    a. Where do you live now?

    b. Where are you going to move?

    c. Where did you live when you were young?

6. My dog Rover has a big appetite.

    a. He sleeps a lot.

    b. He eats a lot.

    c. He looks terrible.

7. My mother is going to mend my shirt.

    a. She's going to wash my shirt.

    b. She's going to give my shirt to someone.

    c. She's going to fix my shirt.

8. I'm going to ask for a raise.

    a. You should speak to your boss.

    b. You should speak to your landlord.

    c. You should speak to your teacher.

9. I was standing in line.

    a. I was the only person there.

    b. There were ten people in front of me.

    c. Everyone liked my pictures.

10. Paul is a teenager.

    a. He's in high school.

    b. He just retired.

    c. He's ten years old.

11. My Uncle George has a Greek accent.

    a. He wears it all the time.

    b. He bought it when he was in Greece.

    c. Everybody knows he's from Greece.

12. Dr. Jones has a lot of patients.

    a. He never gets angry.

    b. He's a very popular doctor.

    c. I know. He never gets sick.

A. BEFORE

1. Mr. and Mrs. Hardy couldn't stop talking about their grandson last night.

   They (visit) __had__ just __visited__ him the week before.

2. I'm sorry I couldn't help you yesterday, but I (get) _____ just _____ back from my vacation, and I had a lot to do.

3. Eric had to study all weekend because he (do) _____ _____ very badly on his history examination.

4. My husband invited some friends for dessert, and he forgot to tell me.   Fortunately, I (bake)

   _____ just _____ an apple pie a few hours before they arrived.

5. Mrs. Martin was very tired yesterday morning because she (give) _____ _____ a big party the night before.

6. I didn't buy any more milk today because we (buy) _____ just _____ some yesterday.

7. Jeffrey looked wonderful when I saw him last Tuesday.   He (go) _____ _____ on a diet the week before.

8. We stopped driving at 10:00 because we (drive) _____ already _____ 400 miles, and we wanted to rest.

9. Timothy was crying when I visited him yesterday.   He (hurt) _____ just _____ himself.

10. Mr. and Mrs. Schultz couldn't buy the computer they wanted because they (spend) _____

    _____ all their money on their vacation.

11. When I got up this morning, my wife (leave) _____ already _____ for work.

12. Sheila couldn't lend me her English book because she (lose) _____ _____ it.

13. Donald looked terrible when I saw him.   His clothes were dirty, and he (grow) _____

    _____ a beard.

14. Katherine didn't sleep well last night because she (eat) _____ _____ a large piece of pizza before she went to bed.

B. LATE FOR EVERYTHING

Joe Richards was very upset yesterday.
He didn't get up until 10 A.M., and he was
late for EVERYTHING all day.

> French class
> begins at 11:00.

> Dear Joe,
> Let's have an early lunch.
> I have to go back to work
> at 1:00.

1. He got to his French class at 11:30.

   It _had_ already ____begun____ .

2. He got to the restaurant at 1:30.

   His friend _____ already _____
   back to work.

> Mrs. Wilson is giving
> a science test at 2:00.

> Dear Joe,
> I'll be leaving at 3:30.
> Hope to see you before then.

3. He got to science class at 3:00.

   Mrs. Wilson _____ already _____
   the test.

4. He got to his friend's house at 4:00.

   His friend _____ already _____ .

> Professor Dupont's lecture on modern
> French poetry starts at 4:30.

> The library will close at 5:00 today.

5. He got to the lecture at 5:00.

   It _____ already _____ .

6. He got to the library at 5:30.

   It _____ already _____ .

> Dear Joe,
> We'll be arriving at
> the airport at 6:00.

> Mary Richards and Edward Thompson
> will be getting married on April 19th
> at 8:00.

7. He got to the airport at 6:15.

   His aunt and uncle _____ already

   _____ .

8. He got to the church at 9:00.

   His cousin Mary _____ already

   _____ married.

C. TOM TOUGH

Tom Tough got out of jail yesterday.   He had been in jail for ten long years.   Before Tom went to jail, he enjoyed:

1. visiting his friends

2. driving his motorcycle

3. going bowling

He also enjoyed:

4. ....

5. ....

6. ....

7. ....

8. ....

Yesterday was the happiest day of Tom's life.   He did all the things he hadn't done in a long time.

1. _____*He visited his friends*_____ again. _____*He hadn't visited them*_____
   in ten years.

2. _____ again. _____
   in ten years.

3. _____ again. _____
   in ten years.

4. _____ again. _____
   in ten years.

5. _____ again. _____
   in ten years.

6. _____ again. _____
   in ten years.

7. _____ again. _____
   in ten years.

8. _____ again. _____
   in ten years.

D. WORKING HARD

Linda was very busy after school yesterday.

| 3:00 write an English composition |
| 4:00 study for my math examination |
| 5:00 review my French lessons |
| 6:00 read the next history lesson |

What was she doing at 4:00?

1. _____ *She was studying for* _____

_____ *her math examination.* _____

What had she already done?

2. _____ *She had already written an English composition.* _____

What hadn't she done yet?

3. _____ *She hadn't reviewed her French lessons yet.* _____

4. _____

Sharon and Roberta were very busy this morning. They were practicing for the marathon.

| 8:00 go jogging |
| 9:00 swim across the pool 100 times |
| 10:00 lift weights |
| 11:00 take a karate lesson |

What were they doing at 10:00?

5. _____

What had they already done?

6. _____

7. _____

What hadn't they done yet?

8. _____

Bobby spent all yesterday afternoon.
making Christmas gifts for his family.

1:00 draw a picture for my mother
2:00 build a birdhouse for my cousins
3:00 write a story for my father
4:00 knit a sweater for Rover

What was he doing at 2:00?

9. _____

_____

What had he already done?

10. _____

What hadn't he done yet?

11. _____

12. _____

E. WHAT HAD THEY BEEN DOING?

1. The Johnsons moved out of their apartment building last week.   They (live) _____*had*_____

   _____*been living*_____ there for several years.

2. Our daughter danced very well in the school play yesterday.   She (practice) _____

   _____ since the first week of school.

3. Jeff was happy when he finally finished his English composition.   He (write) _____

   _____ it for two months.

4. Anita finally took a vacation last week.   She (work) _____

   _____ very hard all year.

5. We were sad when Rudy's Restaurant burned down.   We (plan) _____

   _____ to eat there on our anniversary.

F. WHAT ARE THEY SAYING?

1. Arthur found his watch while he was cleaning his room this morning.

   I'm glad. He (look) _____ *had been looking* _____ for it all week.

2. Julie did very well on her science test.

   Of course she did! She (study) _____ for it all month.

3. Tom looked very tired yesterday evening.

   I know. He (work) _____ all day.

4. George and Eleanor got married last week.

   I don't believe it! They (go) _____ together for only a month.

5. We're sorry you couldn't go on the picnic with us last weekend.

   I am, too. I (look forward to) _____ it for a long time.

6. Why was Martha so nervous last night?

   She (drink) _____ coffee all day.

7. Did Louis go to the beach with you last Sunday?

   No, he didn't. He (plan) _____ to go, but he decided not to.

G. LISTEN

Listen to each word and then say it.

 [r!]

1. return
2. rocking chair
3. practice
4. drug store
5. favorite
6. borrow
7. around
8. restaurant

 [l!]

1. lively
2. loudly
3. glasses
4. violin
5. eleven
6. believe
7. cold
8. fall asleep

81

H. MA__Y__OU'S B__OKEN TYPEW__ITER

Marylou's typewriter is broken. The r's and the
l's don't always work. Fill in the missing r's and
l's, and then read Marylou's letters aloud.

1.

R_obert,
   I'm af__aid the__e's
something w__ong with the
__adiato__ in the _living
__oom. A__so, the
__ef__ige__ator is b__oken.
I ca____ed the __and__ord
and comp__ained. He'____
t__y to __epair both the
__adiato__ and the
__ef__ige__ato__ tomo____ow.
                    Ma__y__ou

2.

__ouise,
   I'm te____ibly wo____ied about my
b__othe__ __a__y's health.   He
hasn't been fee__ing ve__y we____
__ecent__y.   Acco__ding to Docto__
__arson, __a__y is having
p__ob__ems with his b__ood
p__essu__e.   He __eal__y should
t__y to __e__ax and take __ife a
__itt__e easie__.
                    Ma__y__ou

3.

__oger,
   He__e's how to get to I__ene's house.   D__ive a__ong Cent__al
St__eet unti__ you __each the G__eenville __ib__ary.   Tu__n
__ight. D__ive a __itt__e __onger (one mo__e mi__e) and tu__n
__eft at the co__ner of __iver and G__een St__eets.   I__ene lives
in the da__k b__own apa__tment bui__ding ac__oss f__om the
__aund__omat and the p__ayground.   He__ add__ess is Fou__teen
__ive__ St__eet.   I'm su__e you'____ find he__ apa__tment easi__y.
                                            Ma__y__ou

4.

__osa,
   I'____ be f__ying to __ome
on F__iday, and I'____ be
__etu__ning th__ee days __ater.
Can you p__ease d__ive me to the
ai__po__t?   The p__ane __eaves
on F__iday mo__ning at e__even
o'c__ock.
            A____ my __ove,
            Ma__y__ou

5.

A__nold,
   Can you __ecommend a
__estau__ant in you__
neighbo__hood?   I'm p__anning
to take my __elatives to __unch
tomo____ow, but I'm not su__e
whe__e. We've a____eady t__ied
the Eng__ish Tea __oom, but we
didn't __ike thei__ f__uit
sa__ad.   You and G__ego__y had
__unch at an exce____ent
__estau__ant __ast week.   Do
you __emembe__ the name of the
p__ace?
            You__ f__iend,
            Ma__y__ou

Listen to each sentence.   Put a circle around the appropriate answer.

Ex. a. She can't find it anywhere.
  b. Where can they be?
  (c.) We can't hear her at all.

1. a. I hope he feels better soon.
  b. What happened?   Did you twist it?
  c. How are your cousins?

2. a. Did you take a lot of photographs?
  b. I'm glad you didn't fall and hurt yourself.
  c. That's too bad.   I know you were looking forward to it.

3. a. I know.   He's missed all his tests.
  b. I know.   He's been doing very poorly.
  c. I know.   He hasn't taken any tests this year.

4. a. How many miles did you travel?
  b. Isn't flying in airplanes dangerous?
  c. Did you enjoy yourselves?

5. a. What a shame!   She won't be able to sing.
  b. What a shame!   She won't be able to knit.
  c. What a shame!   She won't be able to walk.

6. a. No.   We work for different companies.
  b. No.   She's my aunt.
  c. Yes.   She's my mother's cousin.

7. a. Did you see anything interesting?
  b. Did you buy a new kitchen window?
  c. Did you get everything you needed?

8. a. Was it a very bad accident?
  b. Do you know anybody who can repair it?
  c. How long had you been going out together?

9. a. He's having problems with his teeth.
  b. That's okay.   We all make mistakes.
  c. He's having problems with his feet.

10. a. I think so.   She's been working very hard.
  b. I think so.   The airport isn't very crowded.
  c. I hope so.   She wears them all the time.

11. a. We wrote about politics.
  b. We talked about modern art.
  c. We read about computer technology.

12. a. No.   Where was he going?
  b. No.   I didn't see the bus stop.
  c. No, I didn't.   But I heard the music.

13. a. He's going to have a party.
  b. He's going to go on vacation.
  c. He received a lot of presents on his birthday.

14. a. When did you learn how to sew?
  b. Who are you giving it to?
  c. Would you like to talk about it?

15. a. Poor Patty.   She's always sick.
  b. Poor Patty.   She needs a new pair of boots.
  c. She's too shy.

16. a. I like you, too.
  b. You don't have anything to be jealous about.
  c. What are you going to send me?

A. **Complete the sentences with the appropriate verb form.**

(eat)   1. Why do you keep on _____ junk food?

(smoke) 2. My mother thinks _____ is bad for my health.

(move)   3. I've decided _____ to a new apartment.

(swim)   4. Jim practices _____ every day.

(dance) 5. _____ is a good way to relax.

(play)   6. Where did your sister learn _____ the guitar so well?

(talk)   7. Please stop _____ . I'm trying to sleep!

(get up) 8. Sally thinks _____ early is a good way to start the day.

B. **Complete the sentences, using the past perfect tense.**

Ex. (go) The jazz concert last night was wonderful. I _____*hadn't gone*_____ to a jazz concert since last summer.

(start) By the time Anita got to church, the wedding __*had*__ already __*started*__ .

(speak) 1. I had dinner with some Mexican friends last night. I enjoyed myself because I

_____ Spanish in a long time.

(do)   2. By the time Susan's father got home from work, she _____ already _____ her homework and was ready to play chess with him.

(leave) 3. George was upset. By the time he got to the train, it _____ already _____ .

(write) 4. I wrote a long letter to my grandparents last night because I _____ to them in several months.

(give) 5. Peter didn't give blood last January because he _____ blood the month before.

(wear) 6. I wore the dress my husband gave me to the party last night because I _____

_____ it in a long time.

(eat)   7. I ate a piece of chocolate cake last night and felt terrible about it. I _____

_____ a rich dessert since I started my diet.

C. Complete the sentences, using the past perfect continuous tense.

Ex. (study)   Shirley was glad she did well on her geography exam.   She _____*had been studying*_____ for it for days.

(practice) 1.   Steve lost the tennis match this afternoon.   He was upset because he

_____ hard for the past few months.

(plan)   2.   Mr. and Mrs. Martin didn't go on their vacation because they got sick.   They were

sorry because they _____ their trip for months.

(look   3.   I'm disappointed you had to cancel your party last weekend.   I _____
forward)

_____ to it for a long time.

(argue)   4.   Ann and Jeff broke up last night.   They _____
with each other for the past several weeks.

D. Listen and put a circle around the correct answer.

Ex. (a.) take photographs.
    b.   painting portraits.

1. a.   eating so much ice cream.
    b.   gamble.

2. a.   to take out Betty.
    b.   marrying Linda.

3. a.   to move into an apartment.
    b.   buying a house.

4. a.   taking piano lessons.
    b.   study the violin.

5. a.   to make her own clothes.
    b.   working in her garden.

6. a.   teach history.
    b.   working at the university.

A. WHAT ARE THEY SAYING?

1.

   Did you pick up Rover at the vet today?

   No. I didn't _____*pick him up*_____. I thought YOU did.

2. A. When did the children turn on the TV?

   B. They _____ three hours ago.   They've been watching it all afternoon.

3. A. Has Paul filled out his income tax form yet?

   B. Yes, he has.   He _____ last week.

4. A. Where can I hang up my hat and coat?

   B. You can _____ in the closet next to mine.

5. A. Did Sharon take back her library books yesterday?

   B. No, she didn't.   She's going to _____ today.

6. A. When are you going to throw out these old souvenirs from our trip to Rome?

   B. I'm never going to _____ .   They'll always be very special to me.

7. A. Have your parents picked out their new car yet?

   B. Yes, they have.   They _____ yesterday.

8. A. Has Julia put away her wedding gown?

   B. No, she hasn't.   She's going to _____ after she gets it from the cleaner's.

9. A. Did Charlie call up his mother to wish her "Happy Birthday"?

   B. No.   He didn't _____ .   He forgot it was her birthday!

B. WHAT ARE THEY SAYING?

bring back	put away	take out
call up	put on	turn off
hand in	take off	turn on

1. Why are you putting your pajamas ___*on*___ ? It's only eight o'clock in the evening.

   Oh! I'm ___*putting them on*___ because I thought it was eleven o'clock. I think my watch is broken.

2. When are you going to hand _____ your English composition?

   I'm going to _____ tomorrow morning before class. I have to write it tonight.

3. Have you put your school books _____ for the summer?

   I sure have. I _____ last week. I don't want to see them again until next September.

4. Why don't you take _____ your hat and coat? It's warm in here. .

   I'll _____ in a few minutes. I'm still a little cold.

5. You haven't called _____ your Uncle Henry recently.

   I know. When I _____ last month, he talked for more than two hours. I really hate long telephone calls.

6. Did you turn your heat _____ last night?

   Yes, I did. I _____ for the first time this winter. It was a very cold night.

7. When are the neighbors going to turn their stereo _____ ? It's after midnight!

   I don't know. But if they don't _____ soon, I'm going to call the landlord.

8. Do you think Marylou will bring her boyfriend _____ to the house after the soccer game?

   I don't know. Maybe she'll _____ . I really want to meet him.

C. WHAT ARE THEY SAYING?

cross out	look up	turn down
do over	think over	turn off
give back	throw* away	use up
		write down

(throw, threw, thrown)

1.

   What's the matter with the radio, Grandma?   Is it broken?

   No, it isn't.   I _____ *turned it off* _____ because I couldn't stand listening to that loud rock music.

2. A. Are you going to accept your new job offer?

   B. I don't know.   I'll have to _____ carefully.

3. A. What's Mr. and Mrs. Warren's telephone number?

   B. I'm not sure.   Why don't you _____ in the telephone book?

4. A. Did Alice accept Fred's invitation to the dance?

   B. No, she didn't.   She had to _____ because she already had a date with somebody else.

5. A. Do our neighbors still have the keys to our house?

   B. No, they don't.   They _____ after our vacation.

6. A. What's Donald's new address?

   B. I'm not sure.   But I know I've _____ somewhere.

7. A. Mrs. Smith really liked the English composition I handed in.

   B. I envy you.   You won't have to _____ for homework tomorrow.

8. A. Where's the sugar?

   B. I'm sorry, but there isn't any.   I _____ when I made that carrot cake last night.

9. A. Should I erase all these mistakes in my science homework?

   B. Why don't you just _____?

10.

    What did you do with this morning's newspaper?

    I _____.   Didn't you already read it?

D. GETTING READY FOR A VACATION

Put a circle around the correct answer.

The Grant family is going to go on vacation today.   Everyone in the family is excited because they're going to go skiing for two weeks.   Here are some things they have to do before they leave.

What does Mr. Grant have to do?

1. He has to | (drop off) / turn off | their dog at a friend's house.

2. He has to | take out / take off | some money from the bank for their trip.

What does Mrs. Grant have to do?

3. She has to | hang up / figure out | the telephone and electric bills.

4. She has to | put away / throw away | the laundry.

5. She has to | cross out / throw out | some old newspapers and magazines and | put on / pick up |

some new ones to read on the plane.

What do Lucy and Arthur have to do?

6. They have to | take down / put on | the Christmas decorations from last night's party.

7. They have to | pick out / use up | the clothes they'll need for the trip.

8. Lucy also has to | hand in / give back | the ice skates she borrowed from her friend.

9. And Arthur has to | call up / hang up | their hotel to say they'll be arriving late.

E. HOW ABOUT YOU?

You're going to go on vacation today.   What do you have to do before you leave?

1. I have to _____ _____ my English homework.   My teacher wants it before I leave.

2. I have to _____ _____ my apartment.   It's very dirty.

3. I have to _____ _____ the clothes I left at the cleaner's.   I'll need them for my trip.

4. I have to _____ _____ my vacation address and telephone number and give them to my neighbor.

5. I have to remember to _____ _____ a light in the living room so my apartment won't be dark.

6. Also, I have to ....

....

F. WHAT SHOULD THEY DO?

call up	put away	throw out
do over	put on	turn off
give back	take down	use up
look up	think over	write down
pick up		

1. A. The heat is on too high.

    B. Why don't you _____ *turn it off* _____?

2. A. I don't know the definition of this word.

    B. You really should _____.

3. A. We haven't talked to Uncle Fred on the telephone in months!

    B. You're right. Let's _____ today.

4. A. I can NEVER remember your address.

    B. It's 45 Main Street. Why don't you _____?

5. A. Believe it or not, it's summer and my skis are still in my car.

    B. Don't you think it's time to _____?

6. A. I don't know if we should hire Mr. Stevens or Mr. Sharp.

    B. It's a very difficult decision. Let's _____.

7. A. This English composition I just wrote is very boring.

    B. I know. Maybe you should _____.

8. A. It's March, and my Christmas decorations are still up!

    B. They are?! Why don't you _____?

9. A. Aunt Gertrude is going to arrive at the bus station in a little while.

    B. Well, I guess we really should _____.

10. A. I still haven't returned my neighbor's screwdriver.

    B. You haven't? You borrowed it three months ago. Why don't you

        _____?

11. A. Do you want to see my new fur jacket?

    B. Sure. _____!

12. A. I'm very embarrassed. These are the worst photographs anyone has ever taken of me.

    B. Well, if they bother you that much, why don't you _____?

13. A. We still have half a bottle of soda. Should I buy some more?

    B. Don't bother. Let's _____ first.

G. COME UP WITH THE RIGHT ANSWER

call on	hear from	pick on
get along with	look through	run into
get over	look up to	take after

1. I _____*take after*_____ my mother. We're both athletic, we're both interested in music, and we both like to paint. I'm really glad I _____*take after her*_____.

2. My wife and I have both had the flu this winter. I had it for only one week, but she had it for three. I think I _____ faster because I stayed home and took care of myself.

3. I'm so embarrassed. Professor Kendall _____ three times in class today, and I didn't know ANY of the answers. I've got to study harder.

4. I can't believe it! I _____ my old boyfriend in the drug store yesterday afternoon. And then I _____ again last night at the movie theater!

5. I don't _____ my mother-in-law very well. We often disagree. All the other people in our family _____. Why can't I?

6. I haven't _____ my Uncle Bill in three weeks. I hope he's okay. I usually _____ every week, and I always enjoy his letters. I really should call him up tonight.

7. Why does my big sister _____ so much? I try to be nice to her, but she bothers me all the time.

8. I really enjoyed _____ my old love letters last night. I hadn't _____ in a long time.

9. I really _____ my grandfather. He's honest, intelligent, and very kind. I hope some day when I'm a grandfather, my grandchildren will _____, too.

H. LISTEN

Listen to each sentence.   Put a circle around the appropriate answer.

1. a. blue
    b. $15
    c. large

2. a. Fine.   I'll buy it.
    b. Don't worry.   We have larger ones.
    c. I know.   It's very baggy.

3. a. Everything in the store is cheaper
        this week.
    b. Everything in the store is 20 cents
        less this week.
    c. The store isn't having a sale this week.

4. a. How many pairs of shoes did you use up?
    b. How many pairs of shoes did you put on?
    c. How many pairs of shoes did you buy?

5. a. Was it a bad accident?
    b. That's nice.   You haven't seen him in a
        long time.
    c. Do you like to jog?

6. a. It's too hot in this room.
    b. It's too cold in this room.
    c. It's very windy.

7. a. He's always with her.
    b. They're both shy.
    c. His mother always arrives first.

8. a. He's taller than I am.
    b. I can never find him when I need him.
    c. I want to be like him.

9. a. I'm sure you enjoy it.
    b. I'm sure that bothers you.
    c. You're lucky she has a car.

10. a. Yes.   I put it in the closet.
     b. Yes.   I gave it to our neighbor.
     c. Yes.   We had used it all up.

11. a. Are you enjoying your trip?
     b. I'm glad you're feeling better.
     c. What a shame!   When are you going to
         call the doctor?

12. a. The music was very loud.
     b. Somebody had picked it up.
     c. I already had a date.

13. a. Yes.   Her brother in Chicago says she's
         fine.
     b. No.   She hasn't written in a while.
     c. No.   She has a very soft voice.

14. a. He didn't need it anymore.
     b. It was at the cleaner's.
     c. He found a suit he liked.

15. a. It was easy because the dentist's office
         is near his company.
     b. He had had a toothache.
     c. He was very careless.

16. a. If you don't hurry, he'll probably miss
         his plane.
     b. I hope he hasn't been waiting long.
     c. Did he fall down?

17. a. He turned it on when he came home.
     b. He forgot to take it to work.
     c. He wanted the house to be cool when
         he came home.

18. a. They often disagree with each other.
     b. She doesn't get upset with her brother.
     c. Mary thinks her brother is always right.

1.

I can take a few days off next week.

So _____can I_____ .

2.

I hate to go shopping.

_____ , too.

3.

I'm still getting ready.

So _____ .

4.

I just missed my plane.

_____ , too.

5.

I was terribly hungry this morning.

So _____ .

6.

I'll be starting a new job next week.

So _____ .

7.

I'm going to be late again.

_____ , too.

8.

I've been making a lot of mistakes recently.

So _____ .

B. WHAT A COINCIDENCE!

A. Do you live near here?

B. Yes. I live on Summer Street.

A. Really? So _____*do I*_____. I live in the brown apartment building next to Alan's
Hardware Store.
₁

B. What a coincidence! _____, too. I guess we're neighbors. My name is
Ellen Peterson.
₂

A. I'm Cynthia Blake. Glad to meet you.

B. How long have you been living on Summer Street?

A. I just moved in yesterday.

B. What a coincidence! _____, too. And I've been VERY busy.
₃

A. So _____. Moving into a new apartment isn't easy.
₄

B. Where will you be working?

A. I'll be working at the PRESTO Furniture Company.

B. I don't believe it! So _____. In fact, I'm going there right now.
₅

A. _____, too. We can go together.
₆

B. That'll be nice.

C. NOT THE ONLY ONE

neither/either

1. I wasn't listening to the teacher.

_____*I wasn't*_____ either.

2. I'm not feeling very well.

Neither _____.

(continued)

3. I don't see your wallet.
Neither _____.

4. I didn't get the raise I asked for.
_____ either.

5. I never study for English exams.
_____

6. I haven't skied in a long time.
_____

7. I can't stand working here.
_____

8. I'll never be a good typist.
_____

D. LISTEN: *Coincidences*

Listen and complete the sentences.

1. So ___*was I*___ .

2. _____ , too.

3. Neither _____ .

4. _____ either.

5. So _____ .

6. _____ , too.

7. _____ either.

8. So _____ .

9. So _____ .

10. _____ , too.

11. Neither _____ .

12. _____ , too.

13. Neither _____ .

14. So _____ .

15. Neither _____ .

96

E. WHAT ARE THEY SAYING?

1. Will you or your wife be home tomorrow at 6:00?

   I don't think so. I'll be working late, and so ____*will she*____.

2. How do you and David feel after your ten-mile hike?

   Wonderful! I really needed the exercise, and so _____.

3. Have you seen Fred and Barbara recently?

   Yes. I ran into them yesterday. I was waiting in line at the bank,

   and _____, too.

4. Why weren't you and your brother at basketball practice yesterday?

   I had to help my mother, and so _____.

5. Can Johnny and I stay up late tonight?

   That's not a good idea. Johnny should be in bed at 8:00, and

   _____, too.

6. Would you or Susan like to borrow this book?

   No, thank you. I've already read it, and so _____.

7. Turn off the stereo. I'm trying to study, and _____ your sister.

   I'm sorry.

8. Do you know how to get to Brian's house?

   No, I don't. But William can give you directions, and Richard _____.

9. Should I bring some cheese to the party?

   No. Don't bother. Mildred is going to bring some, and _____
   Ed and Linda.

10. Why are your parents so upset?

    I've decided to ....,

    and my brother _____.

F. WHAT ARE THEY SAYING?

neither/either

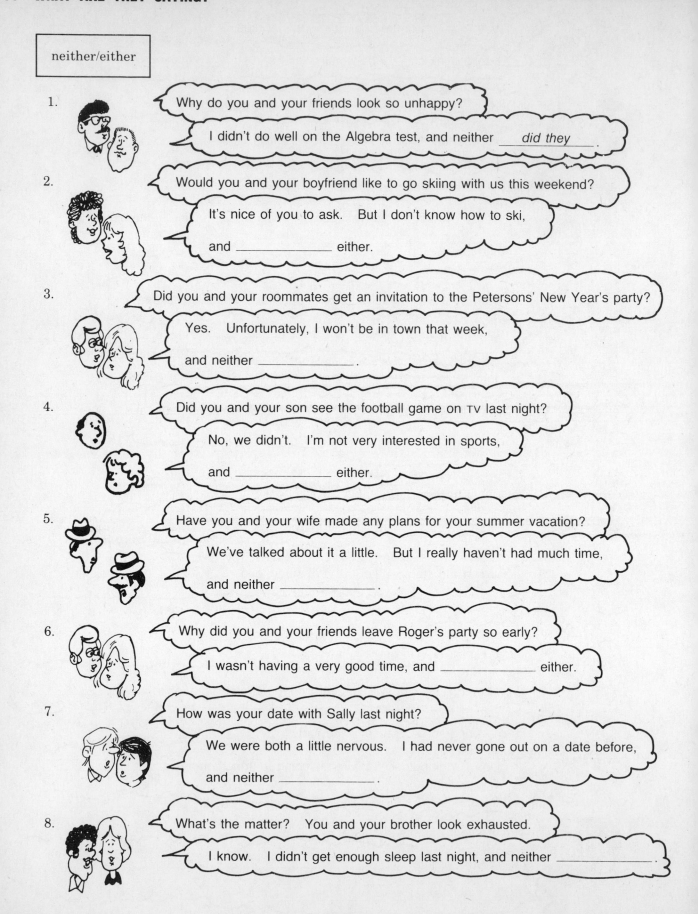

1. Why do you and your friends look so unhappy?

   I didn't do well on the Algebra test, and neither _did they_.

2. Would you and your boyfriend like to go skiing with us this weekend?

   It's nice of you to ask. But I don't know how to ski,

   and _____ either.

3. Did you and your roommates get an invitation to the Petersons' New Year's party?

   Yes. Unfortunately, I won't be in town that week,

   and neither _____.

4. Did you and your son see the football game on TV last night?

   No, we didn't. I'm not very interested in sports,

   and _____ either.

5. Have you and your wife made any plans for your summer vacation?

   We've talked about it a little. But I really haven't had much time,

   and neither _____.

6. Why did you and your friends leave Roger's party so early?

   I wasn't having a very good time, and _____ either.

7. How was your date with Sally last night?

   We were both a little nervous. I had never gone out on a date before,

   and neither _____.

8. What's the matter? You and your brother look exhausted.

   I know. I didn't get enough sleep last night, and neither _____.

9. Should I make dinner now?

There's no hurry. I'm not very hungry, and the children _____.

10. Is the TV still broken?

I'm afraid it is. I haven't been able to fix it,

and _____ your father.

G. WHAT ARE THEY SAYING?

so/too/neither/either

1. How did you and your cousins learn to speak Spanish so well?

I lived in Mexico City when I was young, and { *so did they.*
they did, too. }

2. Did you and Rita enjoy the concert last night?

Not really. I couldn't hear the music very well,

and _____.

3. Can you and your sister go to the movies tonight?

I don't think so. I haven't done my homework yet,

and _____.

4. You and Walter really should order the cheesecake. It's delicious.

I'm sure it is. But Walter can't eat rich desserts,

and _____.

5. Why don't you and your husband stay a little longer? The party has just begun.

I'm afraid we can't. I have to get up early tomorrow morning,

and _____.

6. Why aren't you and Michael good friends any more?

I'm in love with Julia, and _____.

Listen and complete the sentences.

1. but you ___didn't___ .
2. but I _____ .
3. but my wife _____ .
4. but Maria _____ .
5. but my roommate _____ .
6. but my children _____ .
7. but I _____ .
8. but our teacher _____ .

9. but my daughter _____ .
10. but I _____ .
11. but William _____ .
12. but my husband _____ .
13. but you _____ .
14. but my friends _____ .
15. but the other driver _____ .

I. OUR FAMILY

1. My father isn't very athletic, but my uncle ___is___ . He enjoys ___going___ to the
    health club and _____ exercises.

2. I can't play chess at all, but my sister _____ . She's been _____ chess since she
    _____ six years old.

3. When we were young, my brother and sister were allergic to eggs, but I _____ .
    Fortunately, I've always _____ able to eat everything.

4. My mother has lived here all her life, but her parents _____ . They've been _____
    in this country _____ forty years. Before that, they _____ in France.

5. My grandparents sometimes speak to us in French, but my mother _____ . She
    _____ _____ French to anyone in a long time.

6. I'm not interested in math, but my mother _____ . She likes _____ figure _____
    very difficult math problems.

7. I don't have a very good voice, but my father _____ . He enjoys _____ in the
    church _____ .

8. I'll be going to college next year, but my sister _____ . She _____ finished
    high school yet.

9. I've always done well in school, but my brother _____ . He's never _____ a very
    good student.

10. I'm usually neat, but my sister _____ . She never hangs _____ her clothes or _____ away her books.

11. My sister studied Spanish last year, but my brother _____ . He studied Portuguese instead because he's thinking _____ _____ to Brazil on his next vacation.

12. My cousin is a very good ice skater, but my brother and I _____ . We just started _____ a few weeks ago. Before that, we _____ never _____ at all.

13. My mother doesn't know how to knit, but I _____ . _____ been _____ little hats and sweaters all month because my cousin _____ _____ _____ _____ a baby.

J. SOUND IT OUT

Listen to each word and then say it.

full:
1. cook
2. would
3. put
4. foot

fool:
1. soon
2. new
3. Judy
4. food

full!
fool!

Listen and put a circle around the word that has the same sound.

1. full:	pool	(cookies)	shoe
2. fool:	too	could	blood
3. good:	soup	shouldn't	June
4. hood:	flu	suit	put
5. supermarket:	cup	Lucy	upstairs
6. woman:	sugar	true	Stuart

Now make a sentence using all the words you circled.   Read the sentence aloud.

7. _____ _____ _____ _____ much _____ in the _____ .

8. loose:	two	foot	bus
9. would:	food	books	spoons
10. juice:	through	shook	must
11. neighborhood:	who	souvenir	looked
12. cool:	stood	afternoon	pulse
13. took:	good	tooth	fruit
14. boot:	butter	couldn't	Susan

Now make a sentence using all the words you circled.   Read the sentence aloud.

15. _____ _____ _____ _____ _____ this _____ .

K. WHAT DOES IT MEAN?

Write the correct letter in the blank.

_j_	1. afford	a.	afraid
___	2. argue	b.	begin
___	3. consider	c.	do poorly
___	4. continue	d.	fight
___	5. discuss	e.	finish
___	6. exam	f.	fix
___	7. exhausted	g.	friendly and talkative
___	8. fail	h.	give back
___	9. frightened	i.	give lessons
___	10. hike	j.	have enough money
___	11. injure	k.	how much it costs
___	12. lately	l.	hurt
___	13. outgoing	m.	jog
___	14. prepared	n.	keep on
___	15. price	o.	meet
___	16. relax	p.	ready
___	17. repair	q.	recently
___	18. return	r.	rest
___	19. review	s.	someone who doesn't eat meat
___	20. run	t.	study again
___	21. run into	u.	take a long walk
___	22. stand in line	v.	talk about
___	23. start	w.	test
___	24. teach	x.	think about
___	25. use up	y.	very tired
___	26. vegetarian	z.	wait

CHECK-UP TEST: *Chapters 9–10*

A. Complete the sentences.

Ex. Don't worry about your mistakes. You can always cross _____them_____ _____out_____.

I've had the flu for the past few days, but the doctor says I'll get _____over_____ _____it_____ soon.

1. I always forget your address. Next time I'll write _____ _____.

2. My daughter is waiting for me at the bus stop. I have to pick _____ _____ right away.

3. Edward hasn't written in a long time. I hope we hear _____ _____ soon.

4. I'll finish my homework in a little while, and then I'll hand _____ _____.

5. Don't leave your clothes on the bed. You really should hang _____ _____.

6. My teacher didn't like my composition. He says I have to do _____ _____.

7. I don't see my aunt very often, but I ran _____ _____ yesterday at the bank.

8. I want to wear this suit next weekend. Could you drop _____ _____ at the cleaner's?

9. These problems are very difficult. I can't figure _____ _____.

10. Tom borrowed my skates last week, and he hasn't given _____ _____ to me yet.

11. I haven't talked to John in a long time. I'll call _____ _____ when I can get to a telephone.

B. Complete the sentences.

> so/too/neither/either

Ex. Mary just finished college, and _____so did_____ her boyfriend.

1. I'm studying Algebra this semester, and _____ my friends.

2. I won't be able to help you tomorrow, and _____ my wife.

3. Jeffrey was very bored during science class, and his friends _____.

4. Gloria can't stay very long, and her brother _____.

5. I've been taking piano lessons for years, and _____ my brother and sister.

6. Robert took a day off this week, and his wife _____.

7. Ted has never failed an English exam, and _____ his sister.

8. I want to go skiing this weekend, and _____ my neighbors.

9. I'm not a very good dancer, and _____ my husband.

C. Listen and complete the sentences.

   Ex. but his brother _____doesn't_____ .

   1. but my friend _____ .

   2. but my parents _____ .

   3. but his sister _____ .

   4. but I _____ .

   5. but my mother _____ .

TAPE SCRIPTS FOR LISTENING EXERCISES

Page 7   Exercise F

Listen to each question and then complete the answer.

1. Does Jim like to skate?
2. Is Mrs. Smith a good swimmer?
3. Are your parents working late?
4. Do Mr. and Mrs. Jackson live on Main Street?
5. Does Mary type well?
6. Is George a graceful dancer?
7. Is it raining?
8. Are your friends busy?
9. Do your students watch too much TV?
10. Does your sister drink coffee?
11. Is your brother eating breakfast?
12. Are you wearing a sweater?
13. Do you and your husband go dancing very often?
14. Is Gloria doing her homework?
15. Do you have to leave?

Page 11   Exercise B

Listen and put a circle around the correct words.

1. We work.
2. We worked.
3. Alan and John argued.
4. I shouted at my children.
5. We visit our cousin.
6. We played football.
7. I ate a big breakfast.
8. Our neighbors sing.
9. We bake bread.
10. We drank coffee.
11. I had a bad headache.
12. They walk home from work.
13. We studied English.
14. They practice the piano.
15. I wash the dishes.

Page 12   Exercise C

Listen and fill in the missing words.   Then read the passage aloud.

My parents needed a lot of help when they moved to their new house. I lifted heavy furniture for them, and I painted all the rooms. When I visited one day, my mother said she wanted a garden.   I waited until spring, and then I started one.   I planted flowers and vegetables in the yard.

Yesterday my brother decided to move.   I'm not complaining.   I really like to help.   But I think I'll be busy for a while!

Page 30   Exercise H

Listen and answer the questions after each story.

What's Henry Looking Forward to?

Henry is looking forward to this summer.   He and his family are going to move from New York City to a little town in California.   They aren't going to live in an apartment again. They're going to live in a house with a yard.   And after they move into their new house, they're going to get a dog.

1. Why are Henry and his family looking forward to this summer?

2. Are they going to live in an apartment or a house?
3. What are they going to do after they move?

What's Bobby Looking Forward to?

Bobby is happy today because his mother is going to come home from the hospital this afternoon.   Last week she was very sick, and she had to have an operation.   But the doctor says she's going to be just fine.   When she comes home, Bobby's mother will have to stay in bed for a few weeks.   After that, she'll be able to go back to work.

1. Why is Bobby happy today?
2. Why was Bobby's mother in the hospital?
3. What will she have to do when she gets home?
4. After that, what will she be able to do?

What's Julie Looking Forward to?

Here I am!   I'm sitting at my desk in my office, but I'm not working.   I'm thinking about my vacation.   Just think! In two weeks I'll be camping in the mountains.   I won't be sitting at my desk, and I won't be typing.   I'll be swimming and hiking during the day.   And I'll be reading some good books and going to bed early every evening.   I'm really excited about my vacation!

1. Where's Julie?
2. What's she doing?
3. What will she be doing during the day on her vacation?
4. What will she be doing every evening?
5. What *won't* she be doing?

Page 32   Exercise E

Listen to each question and then complete the answer.

Ex. Does Betty like to swim?

1. Is your brother a good typist?
2. Will Mary be here soon?
3. Does Mr. Smith dance well?
4. Did your children visit you yesterday?
5. Are your friends doing their homework?
6. Does Jane have to go home?
7. Will you and Edward be cooking tonight?
8. Did Mrs. Roberts live on Main Street last year?

Page 54   Exercise I

Listen to the story and fill in the information.   Then use the information to answer the questions below.

Roger Baker is a math teacher.   He's been a math teacher for fifteen years.   Before that, he taught science.

His wife, Jane, is a professional violinist.   She's been a professional violinist since she was twenty years old.   She also composes music.   She's already composed two symphonies.

The Bakers have three children: Jeff, Nancy, and Charlie.   Jeff is interested in sports cars.   He's wanted to be a professional sports car driver for the past five years. He's also interested in computers.   He's been interested in computers since his family bought a small computer last year.

Nancy likes winter sports. She's liked winter sports since she was very young. She's a good skater, and she skis very well. She's known how to ski for ten years. She goes skiing whenever she can.

Charlie Baker is only six years old, but he's very interested in math. He already knows how to count to a hundred. He's known how to count to a hundred since he was three years old. He also plays the violin. He's played the violin for two years. When he grows up, he wants to be a math teacher like his father or a professional violinist like his mother.

1. How long has Mr. Baker been a math teacher?
2. What did he do before that?
3. How long has Mrs. Baker been a professional violinist?
4. How many symphonies has she composed?
5. How long has Jeff wanted to be a professional sports car driver?
6. How long has he been interested in computers?
7. How long has Nancy liked winter sports?
8. How long has she known how to ski?
9. How long has Charlie known how to count to a hundred?
10. How long has he played the violin?

Page 65 Exercise J

Listen and fill in the missing words.

1. I've been seeing a lot of movies recently, but I haven't seen any that I've really liked. What good movies have you seen this month? Will you be seeing any movies this weekend?

2. Ted hasn't been driving very long, but he drives whenever he can. He's already driven downtown three times this week, and I think he's driving downtown again this afternoon.

3. Sheila has taken a lot of photographs of her children. She's been taking photographs of them for years. I think these two photographs are the best ones she's ever taken.

4. Mrs. Warren has given three piano lessons this morning, and she's giving another lesson in a few minutes. After that, she won't be giving any more lessons today.

5. Bobby isn't eating his dinner tonight because he's already eaten dessert. Bobby hasn't been eating very well since his grandmother sent him a large box of cookies last week.

Page 67 Exercise F

Listen and fill in the missing words.

1. A. Timothy has been writing since he got up. He's already written more than ten pages. Who's he writing to?
   B. He's probably writing to his girlfriend. He hasn't written to her for weeks.

2. Mrs. Morgan has given three violin lessons this morning, but she won't be giving any more lessons this afternoon. She's been giving a lot of lessons recently, and she's feeling tired.

Page 74 Exercise G

Listen and put a circle around the correct answer.

1. My brother-in-law Tom really enjoys . . .
2. Whenever possible, my husband and I try to avoid . . .

3. Next winter I'm going to learn . . .
4. Every day Carol practices . . .
5. My parents have decided . . .
6. I've considered . . .
7. Are you thinking about . . .
8. I'm going to quit . . .
9. Why do I keep on . . .
10. My doctor says I should stop . . .
11. Jane really likes to . . .
12. Albert can't stand . . .
13. Are you going to continue to . . .
14. Walter doesn't want to start . . .
15. Next semester Gloria is going to begin . . .
16. You can't keep on . . .

Page 83 Exercise I

Listen to each sentence. Put a circle around the appropriate answer.

Ex. Doris lost her voice.

1. My ankle hurts a lot.
2. I just canceled my trip.
3. Roger has failed all his tests this year.
4. We flew our kites all day yesterday.
5. Have you heard that Margaret sprained her wrist?
6. Is Alice one of your relatives?
7. I went window shopping during my lunch hour this afternoon.
8. I feel terrible. Lisa and I have just broken up.
9. Grandfather can't chew this piece of steak very well.
10. Do you think Sally will take a day off soon?
11. What did you and your students discuss in class?
12. Did you see the parade go by?
13. Michael has been writing invitations all day.
14. I have an important decision to make.
15. Patty was going to ask for a raise, but she got cold feet.
16. I envy you.

Page 85 Exercise D

Listen and put a circle around the correct answer.

Ex. Janet likes to . . .

1. You really should quit . . .
2. I'm thinking about . . .
3. My parents are considering . . .
4. Harry is going to start to . . .
5. Sara enjoys . . .
6. I think Professor Thompson should continue . . .

Page 93 Exercise H

Listen to each sentence. Put a circle around the appropriate answer.

1. What's the price of this shirt?
2. This jacket fits you.
3. All of the clothes in this store are 20 percent off this week.
4. How many pairs of shoes did you try on?
5. Yesterday, while I was in the post office, I ran into my old math teacher.
6. Please turn on the air conditioner.
7. Peter takes after his mother.
8. I really look up to my father.
9. My sister picks on me all the time.
10. Did you throw away our last can of paint?
11. I've just gotten over the flu.
12. Why did you turn him down?
13. Have you heard from Betty?
14. George picked out a new suit for his wedding today.

106

15. David dropped his sister off at the dentist's office.
16. I'm going to pick Jack up at the airport.
17. Joe left the air conditioner on in his apartment all day while he was at work.
18. Mary doesn't get along with her brother.

Page 96   Exercise D

Listen and complete the sentences.
1. I was late for work this morning.
2. I'm interested in astronomy.
3. I don't enjoy practicing the piano.
4. I can't figure out this Algebra problem.
5. I took a karate lesson this morning.
6. I'll be busy all day.
7. I couldn't finish the geography exam.
8. I'm going to leave in a few minutes.
9. I just got a letter from Norman.
10. I have to put away my toys.
11. I didn't hand in my homework.
12. I want to go camping this weekend.
13. I won't be seeing Margaret for a long time.
14. I heard from Maria the other day.
15. I've never run in a marathon before.

Page 100   Exercise H

Listen and complete the sentences.
1. I worked hard last night, . . .
2. Linda hasn't been busy recently, . . .
3. I want to enroll in a dance class, . . .
4. You've already seen my new tuxedo, . . .
5. I'll be out of town tomorrow, . . .
6. I'm not afraid of flying, . . .
7. My friends all went to the theater, . . .
8. We didn't get to school late, . . .
9. I haven't eaten breakfast yet, . . .
10. The other students weren't bored, . . .
11. I can't help you with your homework, . . .
12. I won't be at the meeting tonight, . . .
13. I always wake up on time, . . .
14. I was worried about school, . . .
15. I saw the stop sign, . . .

Page 104   Exercise C

Listen and complete the sentences.
Ex. William likes to write poetry, . . .
1. I'm very interested in computers, . . .
2. I won't be home this weekend, . . .
3. Martin knows how to ice skate, . . .
4. Helen just got a raise, . . .
5. I've never been to Europe, . . .

CORRELATION KEY

Student Text *Pages*	Activity Workbook *Pages*
Chapter 1	
2	1–3
3	4–5
4	6–7 (Exercises E, F)
7–8	7–9 (Exercises G, H, I)
Chapter 2	
12	10–12 (Exercises A, B, C)
13	12–15 (Exercises D, E, F)
14–15	16
19–20	17–19
Chapter 3	
24–25	20–23 (Exercises A, B)
27	23–24 (Exercise C)
28	25
29	26
31–32	27
33	28–30 (Exercises G, H)
Check-Up Test	30–32
Chapter 4	
36–37	33–35
39	36–37
40	38
41	39–41
43–44	42–44
Chapter 5	
48–49	45–46
52–53	47–49
54–55	50–51
58–59	52–54
Chapter 6	
62–63	55–56 (Exercise A)
64	56–59 (Exercises B, C, D)
66–67	59–61 (Exercises E, F)
68–69	62–64
70	65 (Exercise J)

Student Text *Pages*	Activity Workbook *Pages*
Check-Up Test	65–67
Chapter 7	
74	68
76	69 (Exercise B)
78–79	69–70 (Exercises C, D)
80–81	71
82	72–75
Chapter 8	
88–89	76
92	77
93	78
96–97	79–80 (Exercise D)
98–99	80–81 (Exercises E, F)
101	81–83 (Exercises G, H, I)
Check-Up Test	84–85
Chapter 9	
104	86
105	87
107	88
109–111	89–91
112	92
114–115	93
Chapter 10	
120	94–95 (Exercises A, B)
121	95–96 (Exercises C, D)
122–123	97
126–127	98–99
129	100–101 (Exercises H, I)
131	101–102 (Exercises J, K)
Check-Up Test	103–104

Note: A Correlation Key for this workbook may also be found in the Appendix of the *Side by Side* Core Conversation Course—Intermediate Level.